I0825158

Praise for

I Would Die If I Were You

A *BookPage* Most Anticipated Nonfiction Book of the Year
A *Literary Hub* Most Anticipated Book of the Year
A *Ms. Magazine* Most Anticipated Book of the Year

"*I Would Die If I Were You* is a reminder that there are intellectual and emotional frequencies that can only be explored through books. In big-hearted, sharply crafted chapter after chapter, Emily Rapp Black dares us to wander through the ways art, reckoning, and sadness are not at all finite, though they are necessarily forever. The writing and ideas here, particularly at the ends of chapters, are just absolutely exquisite. I dare any twenty-first-century reader to show me a writer whose endings are better than Emily Black's. Fuck you, AI. You could never ever do this."

—Kiese Laymon, author of *Heavy*

"*I Would Die If I Were You* is the book fans have been waiting for. Emily's memoirs have never been simply about understanding—they have been about survival. Across love, loss, grief, pain, and fleeting moments of joy, the protagonist we have followed so closely has long felt unresolved, suspended in becoming. This book marks a turning point. *I Would Die If I Were You* is Emily writing not from the urgency of endurance, but from a place of agency, triumph, and power. Survival is no longer the central question; living is."

—Maggie Freleng, Pulitzer Prize–winning journalist and producer

"This book is wise, funny, honest, and immensely generous. Out of all the bitterness and narrowness around us, Emily Rapp Black shines a light and reminds us why honoring our drive to tell our stories is, in and of itself, a way to survive. Like all great writing, this book is full of measures of sorrow and joy that come from experience. And like very few books about writing, it is actually helpful. *I Would Die if I Were You* helped me remember why I want to write, and how to do it more honestly and truly, and I know it will help you too."

—Matthew Zapruder, author of *I Love Hearing Your Dreams* and *Story of a Poem*

"*I Would Die If I Were You* is Emily Rapp Black's greatest work to date—and that's saying a lot. This is a book about how to live fully, how to create art and joy and truth in the world. Through her gorgeous prose, Black imparts wisdom and inspiration. I plan to use her unique (and insane) craft exercises as I approach my own work, and I will keep this important book on my desk, next to *The Triggering Town* by Richard Hugo and Ann Patchett's *The Getaway Car.*"

—Amanda Eyre Ward, *New York Times* bestselling novelist

"*I Would Die If I Were You* is brilliant, profound, and endlessly inspiring. Emily Rapp Black has given writers at every level a tour de force of craft and courage. At its core, this is a galvanizing call for empathy and community, a testament to the power of language and imagination and the impossible compassion of storytelling."

—Bret Anthony Johnston, author of *We Burn Daylight*

I Would Die If I Were You

ALSO BY EMILY RAPP BLACK

Poster Child
The Still Point of the Turning World
Sanctuary
Frida Kahlo and My Left Leg

I Would Die If I Were You

— NOTES ON ART AND TRUTH-TELLING —

Emily Rapp Black

COUNTERPOINT
CALIFORNIA

I WOULD DIE IF I WERE YOU

This is a work of nonfiction. However, some names and identifying details of individuals have been changed to protect their privacy, correspondence has been shortened for clarity, and dialogue has been reconstructed from memory.

First Counterpoint edition: 2026

Library of Congress Cataloging-in-Publication Data
Names: Rapp Black, Emily author
Title: I would die if I were you : notes on art and truth-telling / Emily Rapp Black.
Description: First Counterpoint edition. | San Francisco : Counterpoint, 2026. | Includes bibliographical references.
Identifiers: LCCN 2025052139 | ISBN 9781640096899 trade paperback | ISBN 9781640096905 ebook
Subjects: LCSH: Rapp Black, Emily | Creation (Literary, artistic, etc.) | Loss (Psychology) | Storytelling | LCGFT: Essays
Classification: LCC PS3618.A729 Z46 2026 | DDC 814/.6 [B]—dc23/eng/20251222
LC record available at https://lccn.loc.gov/2025052139

Cover design by Nicole Caputo
Cover art © omar belattar / Stills.com
Book design by Wah-Ming Chang

COUNTERPOINT
Los Angeles and San Francisco, CA
www.counterpointpress.com

Printed in the United States of America

10 9 8 7 6 5 4 3 2 1

For
Julie Coyne,
Gina Frangello,
Annemarie Hauser,
and James Lynch

And for my magical Charlie girl,
always

Chaos Theory
for ERB

The question wasn't whether grief
was a kind of truth; the question
was whether its threat instilled
in us deception. It dwells
amongst deceivers, blowing through
even the mild sheet of bluebells
trembling as one meadow,
a thousand flits of chaos
separating into *not me, not me—*

Which is itself our chaos.

—Katie Ford

Contents

I Would Die If I Were You

Prologue

Love and Death

I keep a Rilke quote above my writing desk: "Love and death are the great gifts that are given to us; mostly they are passed on unopened." This statement is essential, inescapable, beautiful, brutal, and true. We are born to love (which means we are born to grieve), and we are also born to die (which means we were born to live, and boldly). I've been carrying this quote around in my head, my heart, even scribbled on a cocktail napkin folded up in my wallet for a time, but it wasn't until I was in my twenties that I realized what it meant and the lifetime investment it required. And that's when I started to write with the intention and purpose that has changed my life.

Many writers will tell you that their desire to write began at an early age, and that is also true for me: furiously bad poems about the color silver; tales of Winifred the Witch, who drove a VW Beetle and solved rural crimes in Wyoming; an imaginary pioneer woman called Jenny, who hiked up mountainsides with ease, a character that came to me when I was four years old and in a body cast. But these were the glorious whims and fantasies that all children create, because we are all born storytellers. To witness a child telling a story that unravels in their mind and is expressed unedited is to encounter, as my daughter once said, "a giraffe without dots"; the impressive time-travel speed of weasels; bugs that wear leather jackets and fly paper planes; a butterfly that turns into a flower and saves the Tulip Planet. It's the world that tells us we cannot, should not, will not, better not tell the stories that are unique to us, that arrive as gifts when we are not worried about the outcome, or the listener, and when we don't yet understand what it means to be self-conscious or ashamed about what's in our minds and hearts.

For many of us, there comes a time when we need to, we must, we should, we will, and we'd better create—despite what we've been told about who we are or who we aren't, how we think, how we love or who we aren't allowed to love, what we should or shouldn't do or be or become. Because when the world feels so sad and brambly and knotted, only art will loosen the cat's cradle of despair that is part of living with and alongside chaos. Stories told through any modality—music, poetry, nonfiction, fiction, graphic novel, art of any kind—make the chaos bearable, if only for a moment, but those moments add up, and all of them matter, and therein lies the magic.

I learned about "betweenity" from the British playwright and Fulbright scholar Sarah Woods, who visited my graduate class in the fall of 2023. She talked about writers being in a very specific position right now—caught between the old and the new, the marked historical transitions of the world, the state of and/also: a threshold moment suspended between what was and what comes next, a feeling of lightness that helps us feel unburdened, if only for a moment. This in-between space can be uncomfortable because it is challenging—maybe even impossible—to box in or clearly define. The concept acknowledges the challenge and discomfort inherent in change. Although the term is often applied to organizations and teams, betweenity can be applied to creative endeavors and to the creators, who may have thoughts and ideas but no real strategy to implement that melody, that character, that memory and so are held in between the conception of the idea and the doing of it. Betweenity is temporary, however, like all temporal states, and if an artist can manage being inside that liminal space, what's on the other side might be glorious, or it might be a false start that leads to something glorious.

Still, the feeling of being between this and that can feel burdensome, and we all have our unique troubles and worries that art won't immediately solve. Who hasn't been kept awake fretting about a worst-case scenario? Our minds are like horror films, taking us to the edge of what's bearable, allowing a quick look, and then moving away and saying, *Never. Not me.* For this reason, like millions of viewers around the globe, I find *Law & Order: Special Victims Unit* a weirdly comforting show. Each episode's predictable structure, the *bu-bump* that signals the change of scene, the action, Detective Benson—portrayed by Mariska Hargitay, every middle-aged woman's ideal bestie—and the promise that someone will find a way for the perp to be brought to justice or at least someone will deeply care if they remain on the lam. In one episode, a victim of rape confesses to

Detective Benson that after experiencing a huge loss in her life, she thought nothing bad would ever happen to her again, and then it did. It struck me then, and it strikes me now, as an assumption we all make, thinking and believing that if one moment of bad luck or intense heartbreak befalls us, we're somehow inoculated against further hardship. We're not. There is no vaccine for chaos. Artists know this; we dig around in this muck, but that doesn't make it any easier to bear. Our burdens and anxieties feel like mulch, and from them, things can grow. That's the good news.

My first book emerged from the experience of growing up with an artificial limb. *Poster Child* is like a Frankensteinian coming-of-age story, only the monster is the girl, or at least that's how I often felt in my young life: the body that would never belong, no matter her achievements or gifts or humor or kindness. As a child, I was given two books about girls with disabilities: in the first, the narrator dies; in the second, she becomes an athlete. I chose door number two until it, too, became limiting and unsustainable, and I wrote *Poster Child* because I needed to believe there was a middle way of being a woman with a nonnormative body (there is!). I couldn't bear the idea of being Shelley's metaphorical creature for the rest of my life, the person looking in on the lives she'd never have because of the way her body happened to be shaped. Many of the book's reviewers agreed that the book was about grief, which I suppose on some level it was. It was also about sex and joy and travel and books and ableism, and a good chunk of it I wrote on yellow notepads while babysitting a friend's young child at the Fine Arts Work Center in Provincetown. I had been living inside the story my entire life, but I was only able to move it out and slot it into narrative when I was relaxed after the toddler fell asleep, feeling almost easy, my attention soft but alert. I thought, *Let me just take some notes*, and two hours later I had cracked the code of a book that I felt I'd never finish and was tired of thinking about. Now I was living alongside the story and able to see it from a safe but intimate distance. With that new perspective came clarity, confidence, and a kind of freedom I had never experienced before.

After the book was published and had its moment, I felt out of ideas, almost cleaned of any desire to create. I got my first teaching job; I lived in sunny Santa Monica and spent long hours at a gym that overlooked the Pacific Ocean. I made friends and had a boyfriend and then I had a different boyfriend and then I had a husband and then I had a child, my first child, my son. Then I had a new job, in a new state, with a heavy teaching load at an institution in crisis in a town where I didn't know anyone. I read a lot while nursing my son, Ronan, but I didn't feel like writing. The world felt quite narrow with a newborn and a nascent network of friends and colleagues and piles of grading each week.

When Ronan was diagnosed with a terminal illness at nine months old, writing was all I could or wanted to do. I certainly couldn't stand in front of people teaching, not right away, so Ronan's father and I made an appointment with the chair of my department, and I could not lower the mask of despair that was my face, and I did not for many years after, and maybe I still haven't and never will, or maybe it lurks under the other masks we all wear to perform the different jobs we do, the roles we play, the people we are required to be in certain situations. My work friends and my new friends were unbelievably kind to me, to my son; they bore witness to the wretched situation we found ourselves in. I wrote as if my life depended on it, because I understood—without a doubt—that it did. There was no hemming or hawing around should I write today or not; it was necessary. I have talked about how writing about Ronan, alongside him, through his short life, his death, and then the forever aftermath, saved my life. Love and death squeezed together, and both often felt like burdens, but then I looked more and more intently, and they were, as Rilke promised, gifts.

After my daughter, Charlie, was born, out of joy in a new love and with a new child, I again could not stop writing. Different extreme experiences and ruptures, same creative result and wild output. By this time, I no longer feared the electric wanderings of my mind, and I knew to respond to the cues from my body when I experienced what I now call exquisite attention, which is any moment when you are completely arrested by an image, a sound, a line from a poem, a person, a feeling. What draws your attention and roots you to the spot is never an accident, and no observation is neutral.

This holding pattern of attention is a sacred one—utterly grounded, but with a palpable lightness. From one such moment I wrote a book about the artist Frida Kahlo and my imagined relationship with her work and life across time and history and culture—not from an art historian's point of view, but from the feeling I had at the Casa Azul looking through glass at her artificial legs and feet and back braces, the bursts of color and flower and paint. I was arrested to the spot seeing these emotions and desires and regrets and longings transcribed onto objects that only those she loved and trusted were allowed to see. I can still sense people walking behind me, the sweat on my back, the weight of my feet in front of the glass exhibit. What a beautiful firewall of privacy, I thought, for an artist who painted her most vulnerable physical moments and every betrayal of her body or heart, and this got me thinking about what creativity is and does and why it matters.

I've been teaching creative writing for nearly twenty-five years now, half of my life. Many writers will say that the dream is not to teach but to write full-time, to sink into the bliss of just writing, but this I could not do, and it sounds, frankly, awful. Teaching does something else for me, something spectacular that is intensely ethical, moral, even spiritual. To be trusted with someone's story, with the contents of their intellectual mind and creative longings, steeped in their emotional center, and then shared, openly, for feedback, is a privilege and a gift. I love the instant-workshop model, when someone reads something fresh aloud to a group, and there are moments of magic and struggle and uniqueness, all paving a glittery road that I hope they will choose to follow and that the people in the room are charged with helping them build, right then, in that moment.

To create community is never without consequence. Not all teaching scenarios are without frustration and annoyance, and I don't stroll into every session feeling jazzed to take on the privilege of holding space for story and craft, but usually by the end of the lecture or the workshop, I understand that the alchemy of emotion and intellect is what all writing seeks to do, and to be at the center of that construction is truly awesome. Not every student goes on to be a celebrated writer or a published author, but that dip into creativity, I hope and believe, will help connect them with the truth of what Rilke said: that by connecting to both what they love and what they fear, they will live better and more fully; they will give themselves the chance to fail; they will be generous and kind when faced with the stories of others, having been vulnerable enough to share their own; they will take risks on the page and maybe in life, for better or worse; and they will understand that you don't get a free pass from sorrow and despair if you want a ticket to the joy and the light. The one is the gateway to the other, a tunnel you traverse for as long as you're alive. There's no right way to do it, and there's no way to get it wrong. There's only the doing of it, the joy of spinning stories from the core of who we are and what we love and fear and long for, and I believe that we are all born to do this magnificent, sacred labor. A song, a poem, an essay, a portrait: all are spun from the same imaginative gold.

My hope is that this book will encourage you to find the creative impulse in yourself, and that it will help you find a way—*your way*—to open the gifts of love and death, no matter what is found, either treasure and tragedy or the betweenity that exists between the two. I hope you make art that tells a truth that is singular only to you, and that through this process, you are transformed each time you pick up an instrument, a brush, a pen.

— 1 —

I Would Die If I Were You

WHY THIS BOOK

The function of art is to do more than tell it like it is—it's to imagine what is possible.

—bell hooks, from *Outlaw Culture: Resisting Representations*

This is not a how-to or a self-help book, but I hope it will be practical and helpful. This is a book about narrative craft, consciousness, and creativity, all of which stem from curiosity; it is about friendship, love, loss, art, parenting, meditation, God, artistic vocation, the body, grief, philosophy, action movies, and the Bible, and how these experiences and practices and texts and images have shaped and informed and intersected with one another in my life and identity as a writer. Although it is about art and truth-telling, it covers aspects of craft, but with a singular purpose: that everyone understands that a creative, vibrant, and joyful life is possible in the time we are given, knowing how the human story ends, and without entirely caving in to sociocultural pressures of productivity that run counter to the richness and life-giving, spirit-lifting potential of the creative act.

I hope the stories and methods and field-tested strategies I offer here will help you grapple with the experiences in your own life, as the storyteller you are, simply by virtue of being in the world in your particular body at this particular moment in time and history at the particular place in the world where you happen to find yourself. Whatever story within you wanting to be told is valuable. It matters. If you want to express it, you can find the ability to do so, even if the expression or telling remains a secret.

Amitha Kalaichandran wrote, "Creating meaning from tragedy is a uniquely human form of spiritual alchemy." There is nothing so sad or so joyful that an artist can't approach and explore, although you may have been instructed to believe otherwise. I contend that the full range of our lived experiences—told with beauty and truth—creates the confusing, difficult, extraordinary, and sometimes terrifying compost from which rise the stories that serve both the writer and, by extension, the world. Creators are alchemists, and writing is an act of service, to self and to others. Art saves people. I know because it saved me. Maybe you are reading this because a story found you at your toughest moment and helped you hang on for another day. Maybe you believe that the story you want to write might shine that light for someone else. Maybe you're bored and the idea of truth-telling is uniquely appealing. Whatever it might be, your story—and your *life*—is never "too much" or "not enough." Both statements are inaccurate as well as incorrect, proven by the act of art itself, which is made out of and alongside all manner of experience, from the horrific to the triumphant. If you can put a narrative frame around an experience—no matter how wonky or bent or strange-looking—you can bear it, even if you are never able to comprehend it fully. Closure is not a thing, but pursuing creative expression absolutely is, and so is a continuous commitment to engagement with fears, joys, loves, and losses, as individuals and in community, through the work we generate. As Thomas Merton wrote, "Art enables us to find ourselves and lose ourselves at the same time." It is and always will be both/and.

We transcend or transmute devastating life experiences not by overcoming, ignoring, or leaving them behind, but by finding a way to live alongside them and integrate and metabolize them as much or as well as we can, while also kicking back against the structures and systems that may have created them or intensified their impact. We live to tell the story, and art makes this possible. Narrative will always provide unexpected lessons and reveal hidden pockets of insight, comfort, and strength. As artists we can be generous and generative at the same time. This is what I hope this book will encourage you to become: generous, generative, alert, curious, complicated, and—especially—joyful.

Yet the question remains: Why? Why beaver away at a writing project that may never see the light of day? There are so many ways to spend our limited time on this earth (many of which are far more lucrative and comfortable and less time-consuming than making art), so why write a book or a song, why paint or create anything at all? Why be curious about your patterns of thought, and about the epistemological compass that guides you, a.k.a. what you know and how you think you know it and what you do with what you know or think you know? Short answer: it's what makes us human. Art makes life worth living when you practice it, absorb it, or long for it. Art helps us live with meaning, purpose, and joy. Don't be deceived. You can have that life if you want it, no matter what you've been through, no matter who you are, no matter how old you are or what you look like, and you get to decide what it feels like, how it's shaped, what it *is*.

I started writing stories as a means to escape and understand my physical reality. For example, the question "What happened to you?" is one I've spent my entire life answering: in elevators, at the gym, in the street. As a lifelong amputee who wore a wooden leg as a child, followed by a series of progressively more advanced prosthetic limbs into adulthood, my everyday interaction with the world is one where I am asked to explain myself via perceived flaws or limitations alone / almost exclusively. This has shaped my sense of self and identity—and consequently my understanding of my role, purpose, and value in the world—in every significant way.

"What happened to you?" is a slightly more polite way of asking "What's *wrong* with you?"—although I've heard that question too. I was born with one leg shorter than the other, a congenital defect: "An accident," the doctors told my parents, "a fluke." My worried and bewildered parents asked, "But what caused it?"—a question I would ask as a child, and later as an adult. What was the root cause? And embedded in this question, like a series of Russian dolls, are other questions: What is *wrong* (which presumes there is a normal body, a right body, and all other embodiments are deviations)? How can it be "fixed"? Why did this happen? Who is to blame? Knowing the answers to these questions changes nothing about the situation, but we ask them anyway.

Growing up in the 1970s and '80s, I repeated my memorized response to the first question—"I was born with one leg shorter than the other and had my foot amputated at four years old." The statement left no space for anything but a knee-jerk reaction of pity—like a very narrow room, a crawl space under the stairs, a neglected closet in the basement. I became accustomed to that feeling of being squeezed into a space that, rather than being singular and only, felt like punishment. I felt outcast, like the lepers in the Bible passages we read in Sunday school. I believed it was normal, this feeling of being set apart, different, isolated, or—as one of my relatives once said about me at my grandmother's funeral—"made wrong." I did and still sometimes do feel like a ghastly anomaly, an object of curiosity, a *freak*. When I first read *Frankenstein*, I could hardly bear to read the sections where the creature is shunned for the shape of his body, for his abnormal embodiment; in Mary Shelley's brilliantly told story, his body, his form, makes it impossible for people to accept or love him. Shelley, of course, makes it clear that this is not about the creature being wrong or at fault, but about the limits of others' empathy and intelligence, and a failure of the world to recognize difference as an opportunity, not a threat. The writer's job is to change the world, which means first changing one's mind.

As I grew older and began, with the help of writers and thinkers like Shelley and others, to interrogate this narrative of being "made wrong," I replied to the familiar question with "Nothing is wrong with me," and allowed this cryptic response to sit between myself and the asker—part invitation, part privacy wall. Not once, not ever, did the conversation continue; there was never a follow-up question. It seemed that without a problem to solve, without my admission to being wrong or abnormal, the asker's curiosity ground to a halt. I was relieved. No more rattling off the intimate details about my life and my body (Do I shower with it? Does it hurt? Do I remember the moment of losing it?). In this silence, I felt a bloom of empowerment and pride rather than a feeling of being uncomfortably sized up and categorized as one thing, when the shape of my body was only one part of who I was—sometimes one of the most interesting parts, sometimes the most devastating, sometimes an afterthought. When I claimed my narrative, I felt less alone, which in turn made me realize that being singled out as having a "bad body" was and remains the most isolating feeling one can experience. It goes against our human instincts, our basic needs and desires to connect, interact, *belong.*

After my son, Ronan, was diagnosed with Tay-Sachs disease, a rare neurodegenerative illness, I wrote a desperate, middle-of-the-night email to a brain doctor whose information I somehow managed to find online. I explained Ronan's diagnosis and asked the doctor if he could tell me what might be going on in my child's brain. I knew the root cause was as literal and deep as his DNA and mine, but knowing this, I still had questions. Did Ronan know that he was dying and was he scared? Did he know I was his mother? I knew he experienced pain because I saw it register in his body, but did he experience panic, knowing his time was so limited? Was there narrative attached to his pain? Was there an image I might use as a container in which to hold his experience? I received a very kind but short email, the upshot of which was this: even the most advanced neurologists and researchers know very little about the brain. During that time, my identity shifted again—from disabled woman to disabled mother of a disabled child—and this shift again changed every aspect of how I lived and understood and wrote about my life.

All my life I've been hearing "I would die if I were you." Maybe you've heard it too. And yet we're still here. Why? Because in the midst of despair, even in your most wretched moment, you have intuited that story and art-making are not just important but essential. The writing *is* the light. The creating *is* the purpose, in and of itself.

I didn't die! I lived because I wrote and read things that kept me in the world, kept me anchored in the joy of creating and learning, which is a spiritual connection across time and history with other writers, thinkers, musicians, artists, and creators. These essays and books connected me with fellow travelers, grievers, thinkers, grapplers, friends—old and new—and strangers who have been through extraordinarily hard shit and survived, thrived, lived. I continue to live for the same reason.

Of course I *will* die, and so will you and everyone you know and love. A death-phobic culture that insists the pursuit and possible acquisition of money and beauty and power will shift this fact is a massive deception, and a dangerous one if we want to live the fullest lives we can according to desires and values not completely yoked to the constant barrage of messages that say, *Buy this and do this and work like this to get more done so you can buy more of this and look like this and you will live forever.* Nope. The statement "I would die if I were you" is true—we're all going to die someday, everything fades and disappears—but as a response to the story of someone's life playing out in real time, it is rude, unhelpful, and reflects that deeply entrenched fear of death that prevents us from living in and through the stories wrapped around the cone of hot struggle where so many rich ideas and opportunities for beauty and art reside and perhaps even originate.

If you have weathered or are living through an intense experience, you may feel alienated, bewildered, and bereft. The textures of that intensity are as diverse as the crucibles that create it: cancer; limb loss; chronic pain; PTSD; war; disability; mental illness; the death of a child; persistent grief; divorce; living under the persistent and violent threat of systemic racism, ableism, transphobia, homophobia, or patriarchal restrictions; caretaking someone who is dying or ill; financial instability. If you've had any experience that creates a rupture in identity, body, and spirit, then you may have been on the receiving end of withering, isolating—not to mention inaccurate—statements like "I would die if I were you," or its close cousin, "Your life puts mine into perspective and makes me understand how lucky I am," or another ultra-rude crowd favorite, "I'm so glad I'm not you."

I've heard it all. Most of it has been unhelpful, some of it has been devastating, and it's always corrosive. This book offers the opportunity to reframe phrases like this or similar ones for anyone who knows how to kill a conversation at a cocktail party simply by telling the truth about their life, by entering a room in a nonnormative body or with skin that isn't white or with a life-limiting illness everyone knows will be the thing that takes them out. Whatever the case may be, remember that nobody in those rooms or anywhere else is doing anything that you're not already doing. As Leonardo da Vinci said, "While I thought I was learning how to live, I have been learning how to die." In the end, we're all the same, so-called tragic story or not.

This is not a how-to or self-help book with craft talks thrown in. I am weary of nonfiction that tells us how to live, or how to love, or how to write in a prescriptive way. I don't know the answers to any of these dilemmas, and I doubt the writers who claim to know do either; I only have ideas. The late poet Tony Hoagland said this in a class once and I wrote it down and underlined it three times: "When people care to write poems, they pretend to be better people than they are." It's important for the creator to regard the self rigorously, in all its spiky and smooth ways. If a creative life is about working back from the ending that we all eventually face—death—and understanding that each day, no matter how transient and ephemeral our experience, we are allowed to begin again, to engage our world and ourselves in a new way, then we are free. This practice—made manifest through the act of creating—is personal, practical, fascinating, and ultimately transformative. And bonus: *it's actually fun*. I don't know about you, but I've been sad enough in my life and will be again. In the meantime, in the betweenity, I'd like to have some fun.

How can the making of art help us survive experiences that feel unbearable, even unspeakable, and simultaneously remain open and generous to the world and others living in it? Empirically and scientifically, I don't know, but I do know that people have been trying to make sense of the struggles they faced since the beginning of time by making art, song, story. My hope is that every reader will emerge feeling inspired by and supported in whatever creative act they wish to pursue, even if this is just a simple shift in how they engage with the world. Techniques of opening the path to a story or essay are applicable to creating new ways to embody your life and mind, whether you are writing a book or not. To create is to live. And creation requires curiosity—a form of compassion, perhaps its most heightened and powerful form.

An artist incubates art that in turn creates containers for others to enter and be changed by doing so. In this sense, it is an expression of love: of self, of others, of the world, of life itself. As James Baldwin said so perfectly in *The Fire Next Time*, "Love takes off the masks that we fear we cannot live without and know we cannot live within. I use the word *love* here not merely in the personal sense but as a state of being, or a state of grace—not in the infantile American sense of being made happy but in the tough and universal sense of quest and daring and growth." Art necessitates courage—no, not the bravery of real-time battle, but courage to travel to the places in your mind, body, and memory that scare the shit out of you.

In a review from *The New York Times* of my third book, which included the scene of my young son's death from a terminal illness and the wild, grief-y aftermath full of rage and strangeness, I felt the reviewer objected to how difficult and unpalatable—bordering on shameful—she found my life story: "Black's power as a writer means she can take us with her to places that normally our minds would refuse to go. But the narrative also takes us to places we perhaps don't belong." At first, I was angry: How dare this person tell me what I cannot do or how shitty she thinks my life is? How dare she tell me I have dragged the reader to a place where they don't belong, and what does that mean? How dare she tell me to basically shut up? Then I felt deeply embarrassed—by the difficulty of the experiences and feelings I'd described, as if I had chosen them (I certainly had *not*) and thus made the wrong choice because I was a big dumb dummy, which meant *I* was bad and wrong because nobody wanted to go with me to the shit places I had picked out for the *Dharmic Dumpster Fire Travel Guide to Places That Suck*, which I had written by myself. It reminded me of being in the prosthetic fitting room in my early twenties, surrounded by posters of hot, buff Paralympic male athletes modeling their fancy robotic legs and hurdling over something or crashing through a finish line. I also had a robotic leg, was very athletic, had been an aspiring Paralympian and knew plenty of female Paralympians. "Where are the women?" I asked. This was the reply: "Oh, nobody wants to see a disabled woman athlete." I felt like someone had shouted through a bullhorn, *What a pathetic person! Nobody wants that story! Nobody wants to see you!*

And then I thought, *Wait a minute.* I understood that this reviewer had, in fact, perfectly articulated *why* I became a writer in the first place. To write about exactly what I was told I could not: the worst moments, the hardest physical experiences, the most intense crucibles, my nonnormative body, my wrenching grief over the loss of my doomed and perfect boy. This material was *mine* and I could work it in whatever way I chose. I could whip out my own bullhorn and start shouting into it with the truth of my life, and I could do so without apology or hesitation.

I've had a buzz-killing, conversation-stopping personal story since I was a five-year-old girl wearing a wooden leg in a small town in Wyoming, growing up in a house full of socially conscious farm people, itinerant community builders, and avid readers and thinkers who loved and prayed to a very Protestant Jesus and gave money to people on the street or invited them into the house when they had nowhere to go. My parents, raised by single mothers in the rural Midwest of the forties and fifties, sang in a bluegrass band; my godfather was an expert on *War and Peace* and could recite passages to me in Russian during my yearly hospital stays; as a teenager, I marched around with signs at a lot of protests, particularly around the housing of nuclear weapons at sites in the Western United States on what was known as the Peace Trek, and had earnest conversations about the dangers of the weapons of war (although technology born from war would later make possible my bionic leg) while rattling from site to site in a janky Volkswagen van, unwashed and occasionally belting out the words to a Simon & Garfunkel song on the only cassette tape we had; my father took me with him to serve communion to elderly people—usually women—who could not make it to church (we called them *shut-ins* then, and I usually took the opportunity to rifle through their medicine cabinets and try on their lipstick and use anything with a powder puff attached); and I often accompanied him to sit with someone who was dying. He sat with the Bible open in his lap, not reading, but shifting his gaze from the pages to the person and back again, sometimes reading aloud, sometimes not. I knew that when he carefully closed the book, the person was dead.

Who are you? What happened to you? I'm so glad I'm not you! were some of the questions and comments I heard as a kid, exchanges that left me feeling both isolated and lonely as well as examined, under a spotlight, like a rare specimen awaiting dissection, like a *thing* (many of these conversations took place in small spaces: elevators, parties, bathrooms, and hospital waiting rooms). Your story, no matter how difficult, is still part of the fabric of who you are, and if you don't want to feel ashamed of what you've gone through, nor are you asking for a "brave" badge of honor, then you're familiar with the look that falls over a person's face when you're honest about certain details of your life. So much sadness and loss, but also, so much joy and power to be found sifting through the ashes post-conflagration. I think of people who've weathered chaos and survived as those whose lives might be described as de novo events, a term used by geneticists to indicate a rare, spontaneous mutation that is never a good thing, and is in fact often referred to as, quite simply, a curse. But at least it's original. At least it's one of a kind. As an artist, that can be gold.

Going to difficult places is precisely the point of art. Most of the time, we don't have a choice about whether we journey to certain places or not, because circumstances have already landed us in those tough spots, by virtue of the shape and ability of our bodies; the color of our skin and how this impacts the spaces we are told we do or don't belong in; our gender identity; or just the chaos of the world and how it happened to land on us (a diagnosis, an accident, an abusive encounter or relationship, a neglectful parent or caregiver).

At times, I felt proud to write for the broken down and brokenhearted; for those who have felt or who feel cursed by crappy luck, cavalcades of chaos, or a series of bad breaks; and for people who understand that love and grief are intertwined. Like those before it, this book is for people who "go there," by accident or by choice or by whatever experience dropped them in a crap hole, naked, hungry, and without a flashlight or food.

That said, trauma and tragedy are not badges of honor, and we don't need to be grateful for them as "character-building" events. That's bullshit. Facing and dealing with obstacles (note I don't say "overcoming") may create character in narrative and in life, but people are only quick and happy to say that when it's happening to someone else, when it's an abstraction, no matter how much empathy (note I don't say "pity") they're able to feel. We don't need to experience things that almost kill us to make us stronger, but these experiences can act as a source of transmutation. In any case, I knew from that book-sales-killing review that I'd done my job in the service of something larger even than just my story: I'd shed a mask. If "to begin by always thinking of love as an action rather than a feeling is one way in which anyone using the word in this manner automatically assumes accountability and responsibility," as bell hooks once described love, then I'd practiced some self-love, which felt strange and pretty new and also awesome. Acceptance—this is *my* life—is and was protection; nobody needed to think my life was amazing and worth talking about for me to do both.

I believe that art is meant to comfort the troubled and trouble the comfortable. This book is for the troubled. I thank my early book reviewer for reminding me that my project is to resist the temptation of internalizing brutal and untrue narratives as personal truth, and that taking readers to the challenging places is exactly what I'm meant to be doing. I want to help writers, artists, musicians, and other creative actors take me there too, to all the terrifying, juicy, uncomfortable places I'd never go without their guidance, so that I can feel changed, connected, compassionate, and *human*. As bell hooks said, "I will not have my life narrowed down. I will not bow down to somebody else's whim or to someone else's ignorance." No narrow lives, please. Wide-open spaces, open roads, open minds.

I loved the book I read as a child that promised "there is a monster at the end of this book." There isn't a monster at the end of this one, but there are monsters within it. This is the thing about any monster, which Mary Shelley's *Frankenstein* has been teaching us for centuries: a monster is only a monster until you get to know it (the literal "it," or "creature" in Shelley's book). Then it's just a person longing to be seen and understood, longing for connection, longing to be held, someone just like you. And that's where you, the writer and creator at the beginning of this book, come in. Nobody dies at the end of this book. Everybody lives—if not in this world, then in an imagined one, a parallel universe that exists in memory and thus outside of our confined notions of marked-out time, yet achingly real because stories make and remake worlds. The only thing that might die are your doubts that you are built for and capable of this work, which is precisely the point. Those doubts will inevitably rise up, but they are not the truth of who you are or might be.

The intention is neither to romanticize nor diminish the making of art. It's both a challenge *and* a privilege. It won't make everybody love you *and* you might fall in love with yourself. It is difficult *and* it is fun. It is exhausting *and* it is electrifying. An artistic life exists only in the realm of both/and, and it always has been, and always will be, absolutely worth it.

– 2 –

The Great Conversation

CURIOSITY, COMMUNITY, AND COMMITMENT

"Hey, wanna meet up later and go over our Greek homework?"

"Yo, any chance you can read my Kierkegaard essay and tell me if makes any sense?"

"Dude, are you almost done with *Three Theban Plays* so I can read it?"

It was 1992, and questions like this dropped in the hallway of my dorm as often as icicles formed along the eaves of the buildings in rural Minnesota—the clean, sharp kind that you could break off and eat like a popsicle. The air was fresh and freezing; a wild night for me was listening to Neil Young's latest record from start to finish and possibly slow dancing to "Harvest Moon" with my roommate if I could tear her away from her biology book; and all of us classics and theology majors were deliberately housed in this particular dorm alongside a few chem and bio majors who thought we were out of our minds. In fact, we were deep up in them, and it was magnificent because we were guided by three things that make for the writer or thinker a safe and vibrant place where vulnerability is welcome and dissent is okay: curiosity, community, and commitment.

Curiosity, community, and commitment: these are the great pillars of creativity, whether it's a translation of a Greek passage, or an interpretation of Saint Augustine's battles of competing urges (sex or God—who can choose?) as described in *Confessions*, or a close reading of a short story or essay. I had always been curious about who wrote the Bible, and now I knew that it was hundreds of people across thousands of years and not God, as it turns out, which I had never actually believed anyway. I'd always wanted to live in a community of people who liked to read as much as I did, and who wanted to talk about books and why they mattered, how they changed people, and now that's all anyone wanted to do. Over the summer we'd been assigned *The Federalist Papers*, and you'd have thought I'd just won the lottery. I was so excited to talk about this book. I had always been the person who did their homework ahead of time, and now I was free to get up at 8:00 a.m. on a Saturday morning and write my first drafts by hand, which if I could read my own handwriting and didn't have carpal tunnel syndrome, I would still do. Asking for an extension was something you didn't do or didn't admit to doing, the nerdy, overachiever's version of murder—*The OG Law & Order: Small Christian Liberal Arts College Edition.*

For two years, I lived in the Great Conversation, or Great Con, dorm as it was called, where we sat piled up in our pajamas discussing Cicero and Plato, reading classics and ancient languages, and struggling through the entire *Oxford Study Bible*, cover to cover, as ice patterned the windows and snow fell in piles as tall as our shoulders, creating labyrinths we navigated on the way to class. Each time I opened a book written in the time when togas and chitons were as popular as the oversize sweaters and Birkenstocks of the 1990s Midwestern college student (now making a comeback), I felt like that writer was speaking directly to me, teaching me, helping me frame and reframe the world, and shedding light on the thoughts and ideas bubbling up in my brain, and yet how? These words from thousands of years ago, still relevant now. What was this word magic, and how could I learn to wield such a wand? To realize that people had been talking about how to understand life for as long as people existed made my mind feel fresh, as if my brain had swallowed a peppermint patty and thoughts could flow right through. Curiosity is glitter with a magic comet tail. And it also made me feel connected, the opposite of what meditation teacher and psychologist Tara Brach describes as feeling "severed from my own world and estranged from my own being," which is a cause of so much moral distress, individual and collective. My Great Conversation classmates helped me shape, express, and understand the world I'd come from, and fashion the one I wanted to create. It was a new nomenclature of knowing and it was delicious.

None of us could afford all the books on the syllabi, so we divvied up the list and rotated texts on a color-coded schedule posted in the hallway. Trading was fun, as you'd see comments with initials in the margins, and you might respond to one with your own quip or start a new conversation. At the end of the Gospel of Mark in my study Bible (it was on my buy list, so I got to keep it, although it is used now as a fitness block for cycling squats) is a string of comments:

> *Whoa, so earliest Gospel but no resurrection.*
> *—ER*
>
> *Sunday school: all lies.*
> *—KL*
>
> *Easter will never be the same.*
> *—CG*
>
> *Ketchup stain here. Sorry.*
> *—DB*

It was the *Flintstones*/old-school version of today's comment thread, only nobody was an asshole. We were like the monks in illuminated manuscripts, having conversations with one another and ourselves within and about the text, but unlike monks scribbling marginalia in sacred texts during the Middle Ages, nobody drew pictures of themselves with ejaculating boners. Thankfully.

I understood that the human project has always been how to reconcile body, heart, mind, spirit—all of it. How I had understood this up to the age of eighteen was through the lens of a Protestant upbringing that emphasized a personal relationship with a male God and promised salvation as a gift and sacrifice from Jesus if you believed in it and him. This lens became muddied now—disrupted in the best way. A fractured narrative lets some light in, and even if the full reconciliation of all parts of being a person in a body is impossible, the effort is not; it is everything. It IS the conversation across time and culture and history and experience: How do we live with meaning, purpose, and joy? To what ideals are we committed? What and whom do we believe in and why? What the fuck are we actually doing here? Why are some people frequently confronted with extraordinarily difficult circumstances, and other people seem to be on a constant luxury vacation? I don't know, but I'm interested in talking and thinking about these questions and others. I certainly don't want to do it alone.

I was engaged in these discussions with the same group of fifteen people (kids, really) for twenty-four months, which is like a decade in teenager time. We became deeply acquainted with one another's minds and personal stories; we knew what time our parents were calling and on which day; we had a sense of our collective losses and histories, even as working-class and middle-class kids from small Midwestern towns or big cities like Minneapolis or Milwaukee. Nobody had a cell phone or an email address or a laptop, as these things were on the verge of being invented or accessible (my first email dropped that year from my friend Kate, writing from Skidmore College in upstate New York, with the subject line "Hey, hottie."). The showers were giant steel heads flowing into a central drain and divided by flimsy plastic curtains; inevitably you'd hear someone shout, "I'm out of shampoo!" and then hear a bottle rolling along the floor and a "Thanks!" in response. We borrowed each other's dot matrix printers and took turns typing out our essays on the one desktop computer that someone with a rich dad had in their room. Or, if you were feeling brave, you might go to the computer lab and try to press Print at the same time as the person you were crushing on and then just "happen" to be there when their pages were spit out, when you'd pray for a paper jam to extend the conversation. Nobody drank to excess. Nobody smoked regularly. Nobody did other kinds of drugs or probably even knew where to find them (at least I didn't). And nobody was Catholic or Jewish that I knew, and probably 85 percent of us were blonds or redheads with some kind of Irish or Scandinavian heritage or a mix of both, me included.

For me, simply interacting with people I didn't know and who didn't know me or *about* me was a huge shift, and a welcome one. When you grow up as "the girl with the wooden leg" in every small town you've lived in, everybody knows your name, but it was a source of being set apart as different in a deficient way, not a welcoming moniker. There were no amputee models with robotic legs in Target ads (which my dad now takes photos of on his cell phone and sends to me five times "to be sure they went through. Dad," usually sent upside down). I was just different and weird, and it was obvious. I wanted nothing more than to blend in, and in this homogenous-looking think tank that was like an Ingmar Bergman film set on a leafy hill with very little sex or cursing, I did. Or at least my brain did, and that was good enough for me at the time. As my cruel grandmother liked to say whenever she looked at my wooden leg or looked at me at all, "It's a good thing you're smart." And, as it turns out, I was. She wasn't wrong about that.

This shared experience of writing and thinking and talking about ideas, all while living in close community marked by respect and tenderness and some old-fashioned Protestant ideals I'd grown up with—bring people soup and crackers when they're sick; be kind by default; help people when you can, even when it's inconvenient—changed my life. We were curious, nerdy, and—most importantly—thinking and living together. We taught each other how to think, and we learned how to think and care for one another in that process. This was our epistemological compass, and it was a reliable one. As Hegel might say, we were a community of people coming to know ourselves in the process of coming to know what it means to be an individual person in a community of people. Up and down the spiral of knowledge acquisition, with each swivel a necessary turn in the path of evolution. To this day, each time I step into a classroom, I think of my two years with that group of people—how well we knew each other, how respectful and kind we all were to one another, how much we laughed and learned—and hope that I can create a similar environment over the course of a quarter or a semester or a few weeks or even a few hours. I want us to have a great conversation about the living text that is before us, whether that's a published essay or book, or an essay or chapter draft that we are charged with ushering to the next level in a writing workshop—together, as a group, like a band of literary elves.

But first I had to learn how to teach, or at least how to talk to a group of people about writing. In 2004, as a recent MFA graduate living as a winter fellow at the Fine Arts Work Center, I taught my first workshop in a primary school in Provincetown, Massachusetts, during one of the snowiest winters on record. The school was on a hill, and sometimes on the drive home I'd take my foot off the brake and let my Buick do long, slow circles to the flat part of the road and hope I had enough gas to make it across town.

On my first day at the strawberry-free school, due to someone's intense allergy, which was indicated by the photos of crossed-out strawberries that lined the hallways like LOST CAT or WANTED posters, I made my way past the cafeteria to the first-grade classroom for my first session. I was nervous, sweating inside my many wool layers and a terrible hat I had knitted myself but wore anyway because I'd worked so hard to finish it.

There, arranged in a circle on chairs designed for children, sat two women holding hands, a man with blond hair, two men who were dressed like fishermen, and two older women, all holding the book I'd assigned, the O. Henry Prize short story collection from the previous year. I almost walked out. The room was silent, and it was clear that everyone in this room was so different from one another, so unlike the groups I had encountered as a student, when the rooms were filled with people of a similar age, class, and color (graduate school included). But, as ever, I needed the money, however small the amount, and I also wanted the experience. I smiled my entering-a-church-potluck smile I'd perfected as a pastor's kid that telegraphed *I am totally open and kind and ready to sample every casserole and Jell-O creation lest I offend the person who made it. Who made that strangely shaped brownie? Bring it here!* I hoped my nervousness would come across as pure enthusiasm. Everyone smiled back. "I loved this book!" said one of the fishermen. "I've been waiting to write my whole life!" said a woman with gray hair in a sweater that was clearly handmade but actually beautiful. Everyone nodded. Everyone returned my smile.

I never should have doubted the power of story. I should have had more faith in the role of community to make those stories live.

What I learned and practiced over those next ten weeks set the foundation for the way I still teach today. Before I sat down and took off my hideous hat, I thought, *Act like it's a Great Con study group*, and that's what I did. I thought, *Be curious, treat this as a community waiting to happen, and be committed and compassionate to whatever unfolds.*

We read the texts, we engaged with them, we challenged them. We also wrote and shared about our lives, and in this small town on the tip of Cape Cod during a winter that brought inches of heavy snowfall that froze in apocalyptic-looking waves along the beaches, we heard about addiction, finding love, living with HIV, long days on the boat for not enough money, coming out as queer to conservative parents who disowned us, and losing older parents after a long period of caretaking with inadequate resources and crappy health care. These students of life and art wrote about gaining a sense of dignity while living with a stigmatized illness, about the sorrow and joy of empty nesting, about cancer diagnoses and economic hardships and alienation from family and friends and children. Inside that room existed all the systems that drive and create story: racism, ableism, classism, sexism, homophobia, patriarchy. And the people gathered in that small space with a clunky heater and without a strawberry in sight, wrote essays and stories that punctured and complicated and challenged each of these systems, and every story mattered to the person, to the people listening and reading, and to me. I loved channeling the energy of the room; I loved listening and asking questions and making suggestions and being able to see how the story was coming together and asking if that resonated with the author and then talking around that for a minute. Each week my ease and joy of teaching grew, and the nervousness left me for good, like a nasty rash that never returned.

I was writing my first book at the time, and after the end of the ten weeks, I walked into the classroom with excitement and anticipation, but the place was already lit and bubbling, as this group of people had fully embedded themselves into one another's lives, at least for this designated time slot each week. You could have popped a champagne cork in that room, and it would completely match the vibe.

After our last meeting, as I was swirling down the hill in my shitty car, I started to cry, which was something I used to do a lot more easily than I do now. I wasn't sure I would ever finish or publish a book, as I had not yet done so and I didn't think I was working hard enough because I never thought I was working hard enough, even when I was working too hard, but I knew now that I loved teaching, and that it suited me. I cried out of relief; no matter what, I'd have something to do with myself. Not a backup plan so much as an addition to the plan that was still taking shape. It wasn't "those who can't write, teach," or whatever rude thing someone had said to me that I'd worried would be my apparently shameful truth. No, it was "those who write get to teach too." It was both/and, or at least it might be. There was no shame at all in teaching as a writer, only fun and meaningful labor, and a fair bit of wonder. Once you get to know their real stories, their true burdens and heartbreaks and best moments, most people are pretty awesome or on their way to revealing that they are. I'd always believed that because I was *taught* to believe that, but this first teaching experience only confirmed it for me. All my subsequent teaching experiences—even the frustrating ones—have only strengthened this belief.

When I arrived at my Work Center cottage to lead my ancient, blind, and incontinent dog into the snow for his evening outing, I found the printed-out pages I'd given to another fellow in that year's group, Viet Thanh Nguyen, who was at the start of what would become a spectacular career, slipped under my door (he also stapled them for me). His notes were meticulous and probing, generous, encouraging, and critical in the kind of way that makes you believe you can solve whatever isn't working. He had spent so much time away from his work to attend to mine. It was such a gift, and it was such a testament to his own belief in the power of story to create and sustain community. The way he critiqued that first set of fifty pages was instrumental in how I still approach my students' work: See what the writer is trying to do and try to help them do it in a way that is beautiful and true and in service of the story. Be generous. Be encouraging. Be firm about what's compelling and honest about what isn't. Also this: Be willing to be wrong. Whether you're critiquing your own work or the work of another, know that your particular lens of interpretation, or "how the world is for me," is created by your individual and unique experience. This lens can be a reliable editor, but also—as with any interpretation—not the only one. Writers aren't doctors: We make suggestions. We don't write prescriptions. We are called to be insightful and generous, as Viet was to me in those shaky first pages of what would become my first book, and as all my teachers have been in various ways.

The goal of a teacher is not to be in charge of dispensing advice and instruction, but to be in conversation, as a reader is with a text, listening and asking questions that lead the writer to the heart of their stories; which is to say, lead the writer to their heart, where all the power originates and where the emotional stakes are interesting because they are always high. All art is, after all, a collaboration, a think tank between writer and reader, artist and observer, song and listener. Teaching is a true heart-to-heart through the medium of a crafted narrative. If you give someone a suggestion and they say, *No to all this hooey; go away,* then that's what you do; you go away and let them sort it out for themselves, leaving the door open for future questions and conversation. Ultimately, artists are allowed to make their own choices. If the reader or viewer or listener doesn't like the result, they also have choices: close the book, don't look, take the needle off the record.

Curiosity, community, commitment. These are the pillars of a creative life, and I would argue that it's impossible to have one without some of the others. Through the adherence to these pillars, we create sacred spaces where art is born and where people feel uplifted, acknowledged, and understood. It's possible to be critical while also being kind. Nobody was ever browbeaten or shamed into being a better writer (or a better person). *Tough love* is just another term for *abuse.*

For twenty years, since that first workshop in P-town in 2004, I have taught hundreds of undergraduate and graduate students, adults and kids and teenagers and veterans in institutions, hospitals, and community classes, in church basements and hotel conference rooms and yoga studios and living rooms and cat cafés. I have sat in light-filled rooms in Ketchum, Idaho; rooms filled with brightly colored chairs in Querétaro, Mexico; and in Zoom meetings during the pandemic, listening to human stories of sexual trauma, the effects of childhood poverty, gender discrimination, a near-death miscarriage in Texas due to its misogynistic laws, breast cancer, and the deaths of children and parents by suicide. This community work is where a great deal of my teaching heart lies, outside of academia and anchored in the experiences of ordinary people with extraordinary lives, because in the end, that is ALL of us. What I know from these experiences is that each and every person in those spaces, live or in a Zoom meeting, sitting at desks or on yoga cushions on the floor, has a story that is sui generis.

Although this phrase is rooted in the Latin form *gener-* or *genus*, which can mean "kind," "birth," "class," etc., with offshoots including *generate*, *generous*, *gender*, and others, *sui generis* has been used to describe singular things since the early 1600s—first in scientific contexts to describe diseases, substances, rocks, etc. that were unique and the sole representative of a class or group. But as it happens in the evolution of language, by the early 1900s the phrase *sui generis* began to migrate in meaning beyond the scientific and legal realm, and may now indicate anything that stands alone, that is singular and only, unrepeatable, wholly unique.

It is both true and not true that there exist stories that have already been told. Yes, our human experience and spectrum of emotions aren't limitless. But if you believe, as I do, that every person has value, then by extension, so is the story they live from the first day of their life to the last.

Friedrich Nietzsche, the great, grumpy alchemist of humor and despair, once characterized art "as a saving sorceress, expert at healing." It is my belief that all stories that have been written, are being written, will be written, will never be written, weren't allowed to be written, and were written and then destroyed are all in conversation with one another across time and history. We are mysteriously connected by story as intimately and scientifically as we are connected to the fabric of our bodies and the body of the world. It's analogous to Carl Sagan's statement that "the nitrogen in our DNA, the calcium in our teeth, the iron in our blood, the carbon in our apple pies were made in the interiors of collapsing stars. We are all made of star stuff." Stories about what makes us extraordinary and ordinary have the power to serve others by showing us who we truly are or might yet be or do not wish to become.

What a gift.

– 3 –

The Only Light Is in the Telling

NIGHT TRAVELERS AND TORNADO THEORY

Life's waters flow from darkness.
Search the darkness, don't run from it.

Night travelers are full of light,
and you are, too; don't leave this companionship . . .

The moon appears for night travelers,
be watchful when the moon is full.

—Rumi

"This entire street here and all the houses on it—totally wiped out. Just *gone*." My oldest cousin, Kate, is showing my daughter, Charlie, and me the path of the tornado's destruction. It's mid-January in Washington, Illinois, and the sky is a low ceiling of gray, the trees are leafless, the air so bitterly cold it's painful to breathe. Yesterday we buried Kate's father, my uncle and my mother's brother, on a day with the same color sky under soft sheets of continuous rain. I stood next to my mom, who trembled as the priest swung the incense over the casket that had just been sealed. Outside, standing under umbrellas, we watched the hearse drive down the quiet street, empty of cars, but with a few people standing on their porches with their heads bowed in respect.

"All of the houses?" Charlie asks, making a heart on the window in the fog from her breath. I see her ten-year-old mind work to imagine it. "Is a tornado like a vacuum?" Yesterday was Charlie's first funeral, first open casket, first time in a Catholic church, and I was worried about how she might respond, what she might think. She was, as ever, curious, and kind. She looked at my uncle lying peacefully in the casket and touched his hand; she shook hands with strangers in the reception line that went on for hours; and when my mom began to cry, she shimmied in front of me in the pew and glued herself to my mom's side and said, "It's okay, Granny."

"Kind of," Kate says in answer to her question. "And on this street, yes, I think it was a bit like that," she says, driving slowly past houses that all resemble one another and look relatively new. A giant inflatable snowman is pitched to one side in the wind; a few mechanical deer covered in unlit Christmas lights move their heads up and down; a man is packing up his nativity scene and lifts a hand in greeting. "One street over," Kate says, "no houses were touched. Weird, right?" Her curly hair clings more tightly against her face in the humid air.

"So weird," Charlie says, "and so rude."

During that historic 2017 tornado in rural Illinois, with record wind speeds of up to 180 mph, my uncle and aunt lost their home. They were clinging to the shower rod in the bathroom when the roof was lifted off and Frisbee-d away; all that remained was the pendulum from the grandfather clock that had kept time in their living room for over forty years. In the news coverage, Josie, then fourteen, the daughter of my youngest cousin, Kerry, was with her father and can be heard crying as the phone camera pans through the wreckage of their house, which now has no roof and looks kicked-in. An elliptical trainer looks like a crashed spaceship. The windows and doors are gone, and wind rushes through the open roof with enough force to rattle pieces of glass on the floor. "Our house is gone," her father says in disbelief, and Josie says, "What are we doing to do?" in a voice vibrating with her youth and her fear.

In the space of only minutes in this small town near the even smaller town where my parents grew up together, all the towns like tiny dots connected by straight roads through flat fields, the world was irrevocably changed and would never be what it once was. This event was—in every significant way—a moment of deep change, or what I like to call, for narrative purposes, a moment of rupture.

Many people begin to write or create after a moment of rupture, which is often a traumatic one: a forced push into the cave, the heat and pressure of the crucible intensify, a boulder in what was thought to be a straight path, unexpected rocks in the river. Heartbreak, loss, humiliation, defeat. It can also be a burst of unexpected joy: the birth of a child, falling in love, feeling healed, a glorious view from the top of a mountain.

A tornado—both the shape and the manner of its movement—is one fitting image for what it feels like to experience rupture. Most people don't survive standing in a tornado, but at least two men lived to talk about what it's like to be on the inside of chaos. In June 1928, on his Kansas farm, Will Keller stood trapped inside the spinning cone, later reporting that everything was "still as death." The ravaged sky was visible through the circular opening, and the walls were alive on all sides with zigzagging lightning and more tiny tornados spinning off in all directions like fast-moving sparks from a downed electrical wire. Twenty years later in Texas, Roy Hall told reporters that the interior wall of the tornado looked smooth, with other twisters breaking free in the bluish light created by lightning that allowed him to see everything clearly.

Grief, one of the most powerful ruptures, is the emotional version of a violent, rotating column of air, and it might also be described as an experience with a strange sense of peace at its center. The experience is unwieldy, disorienting, and unpredictable. It is lonely and visceral, much like standing in the middle of that strange quiet place while being surrounded by danger and chaos and even imminent death. Grief is lonely and visceral—inconsistent, swirling, turbulent—the OG life tornado, if you will. In some ways, grief is the ultimate training ground for a writer. Why? Because the experience is wild and variable and inextricably linked to love, and if creativity is about taming chaos to create some kind of shape, to put a frame around a story in order to bear it, then standing in the center of chaos allows someone to find a clear zone without debris or rain, a space characterized by a calm courage, the bravery of stillness where the only thing to do is observe.

Tornado Theory, as I like to call it, is a metaphorical way of approaching subjects or experiences in our lives that seem absent of light or goodness—stories that I believe require a different angle of approach. On its face, a tornado is a lethal and fearful cone of howling wind, an instrument of destruction. A tornado can kill you, and anyone who has ever grieved at some point has probably felt as if they were dying from the pain of grief—I know I have. But as those who have been inside tornados have reported—with an astonishing symmetry in their descriptions—there is clarity of vision, and a chance to observe exactly what the world has placed around you, literally, by dropping a tornado on your life. If we view a tornado metaphorically, we can imagine that inside the swirling cone of chaos, there is something for you to notice, to use, to take with you if you are calm and still and deeply observant. In this imaginative exercise, nobody dies in the tornado, but they do leave with acute observations and gifts that will serve their narratives. I don't think clouds have silver linings, but tornados do have pockets of stillness. That's a win.

The tearful question asked by my cousin's daughter, "What are we doing to do?" is exactly the response people have to a moment of rupture. Writing about subjects that change our lives is a lot like standing in a tornado. You are pinned inside something that is beyond your control, and asked to observe, not freak out, and then report back your findings. You are a private investigator of utter chaos.

When I wrote the book about parenting my son with a terminal diagnosis, I received hundreds of letters and emails from mothers who had lost children or were caretaking a terminally ill child. They sent photos or poems and even a few pressed flowers from wherever they were writing from. The letters were raw and wild and uplifting in their brutal and terrible truth. They were written on the floors of hospitals, typed out on phones while sitting next to their child in bed, and almost all with a time stamp indicating that they'd been sent between the hours of midnight and 5:00 a.m., the witching hours of vigil when you have a terminally ill child. The bad shit always seems to go down within that five-hour window when the only light is hospital fluorescent, the worst kind of bulb. I doubt I'll ever read the letters again, but I'll never discard them.

How does writing work in a world where one moment there's a fire, the next fierce rapids, then waves, an earthquake, a hurricane, and even now a hurri*quake*? The next moment, there's a still, sunny pond that must also be navigated and traversed. I have never been more dangerously lonely than in the acute moments of my grief, in part because no feeling had any sort of on-ramp. Every moment felt like a doomscroll of individual and world disasters at warp speed: *This now this now this what about this and this and this.* I felt anchored to nothing, and to everything at the same time. A feeling of total disorientation. A rocket into grief space, only I was an astronaut who didn't know how to work any of the controls, and my space suit was faulty and ill fitting. I could not do this alone.

My instinct was: get everyone together and see what happens in community. Why should we be standing in these wild cones of grief and confusion all alone? That didn't feel right; it felt horrible and unsustainable. It had been my experience that if you told people that had *not* lost a child that you were writing about this topic in workshops or writing groups, especially as a mother, they often said, "I would die if I were you," which I didn't think I could hear one more time without losing my shit. (I still have not perfected a response: "Nope, still here"? "Sorry I didn't meet that particular expectation and actually die"? Therefore: this book.) While "I would die if I were you" is a rude, inaccurate observation, "We would all die without community and friendship" feels spot on. I sent out a call to women who *had* experienced child loss who might want to join a writing group. I was thrilled when people answered—a few I'd known through my preexisting networks of parents who had lost children to the same disease that killed my son, but others were friends of friends, or friends of a student, or friends of a friend of someone who thought such a group might be helpful.

In 2018, we met in Palm Springs at a friend's sunny and spacious home. We were eight, initially: from Washington, Vancouver, Oregon, Arizona, Louisiana, California, and Texas. Practically strangers to one another, we had a singular, powerful experience in common: each of us had lost a child. The litany of horrors included Tay-Sachs disease, other congenital conditions, a murder, an auto accident, three suicides, a stillbirth, and leukemia. Three days later, we were familiar with the minute details of the individual crucibles we'd survived.

I had a whiteboard, they had their stories, and during that weekend, many of the exercises and strategies I write about in this book were born, simply by listening to the stories these women told, watching how they struggled to tell them, sensing the release they felt in the telling, and providing that container of listening, supporting, and loving as they wrote. It was, no doubt, a sacred space.

We nicknamed our group the Loss Ladies, and it continued to grow and change shape. Children are dying all the time, every day, in all kinds of ways. This can be hard for us to acknowledge; like most things that are deeply true, there's brutality to it. When I think about the role this extraordinary group of women has played in my life, I think of Ivan's desperate observation in book 5 of Dostoevsky's *The Brothers Karamazov*: "If the sufferings of children go to swell the sum of sufferings which was necessary to pay for truth, then I protest that the truth is not worth such a price."

Like Ivan, we mothers were interrogating our circumstances, born of chaos and chance and other uncontrollable forces we may have thought we could control, until we couldn't: *How is it possible for a child to withstand so much pain? For that matter, how much are we mothers able to bear?*

The suffering of children has been a philosophical and emotional bugaboo since the beginning of time. Dostoevsky interrogates the idea that suffering is needed to "earn" harmony in heaven ("solidarity in sin," a.k.a. "no pain, no gain," Christian-style), and how it should not and literally cannot apply to the suffering of a single child. Not one baby or toddler or kid or teenager or young adult—and everyone, of course, is somebody's baby, so you might extrapolate this suffering to include any and all human suffering. The upshot: if you are hell-bent (or heaven-bent, in this case) on making children fulfill the pact that suffering is required for retribution and access to the heavenly realms, then the whole system falls to pieces. That philosophical house you believed was as old, solid, and true as the world is a Goldfish cracker left to drown in a glass of milk.

I do not believe in a "worse" loss in terms of a strict ranking on some scale, like an escalator of sadness that spirits you into "best of" status or positions you at the top of the grief game. Nobody is keeping score. Grief isn't baseball or bowling. I do believe that how we engage with the loss of children—ours or the children of others—is and should be different, and that the sharing of this loss, regardless of our very different lives, leads to friendship that sustains like no other. The Loss Ladies ranged across the decades: from thirties to sixties. We were married, divorced, single, remarried, re-divorced, partnered in nontraditional ways. We were and are much more than these descriptors, of course, and we are all writers, and we are all mothers, and we deepened these aspects of our identity through our shared intellectual mentorship and shared emotional losses. As much as our group was about loss, it was also about love, and the way a knowledge of one deepens the other.

Before and during the pandemic, this group of mothers was like the single pipe still rooted in the ground during a tornado that means you don't get sucked into a cone of dust and broken furniture and scary wind. I clung to it. One wall of my house is full of photos of the group's lost children; I pass by it every day and look at my son's face at the center of that precious collection of faces. In this group I never would have wanted to join, I found a pure, unexpected love (as nobody expects to lose a child), born of friendship, suffering, support, vulnerability, and dedication.

I am not good at many things: cooking, cleaning, math, patience, spreadsheets, directions, saving money. I couldn't read a fucking map if it spoke to me. I've rarely seen a cute dress in a shop window that I did not buy. But I am a good friend. In friendship, all that I am or am not can be held without judgment, and of course this has never been more evident than in the years after my son's diagnosis, followed by his prolonged illness, death, and then the aftermath of grief that never ends but just changes shape or location or intensity. At some point, grief is no longer driving the bus the wrong way on a one-way street or trying to mow down pedestrians or haul ass up a mountain with an empty gas tank. Eventually, you're behind the wheel again. All my life, I've been told to "be still," or "calm down," but during those years of caretaking and hospice and beeping machines and gutting sadness, I was a person with her head on fire, on a massive scooter or turbo skateboard, revving around the neighborhood just to make noise. Just to feel alive. The grief blaze allows for no feelings to be tamped down; if the fire goes out in these moments, you go with it. I had my writing. I had my friends. I didn't die, and I continue to live and to love.

No heart of stone here, but when it comes to mothers of sick or dying or dead children, when we talk about them—which we do because that is a way of keeping their memory alive, a way of preserving and embracing this part of our identity, the mother part—people are often taken aback, amazed, and sometimes even horrified and judgmental.

"How can you talk about your child without becoming emotional?" Read: *Are you a human being or are you instead an icky robot person who has a mechanical heart instead of one with chambers and valves pumping blood? Like, how are you even alive? You're scary. You make me nervous. I would die if I were you, so you should be dead. Please go away.*

So, first "Be still and calm down," and then "You scare me, so please go away." No. We will not. Mothers of lost children know that when a mother gets thrust over that line and her child is gone for good, the world cracks open and *whoosh*, into the pit she goes. It doesn't matter how many people loved that mother or her child, she's alone in there, screaming and howling—not forever, although it will seem like forever—and that is where she is asking about the suffering of children, no matter her religious or spiritual beliefs. She is asking to suffer instead, to die instead, but she knows there is no way to suffer more than this. It will do no good to continue this discussion with God, the universe, Buddha, what or whomever. Now she is stoic and exhausted, and she starts looking around for a way out of this weird hole. Her crying stops.

All this time, other women—mothers and others who are not mothers but who love this mother—have been tossing ropes and flashlights from above, and they are not stoic at all. They are hysterical in the truest sense of the word—all with their uteruses and femaleness or perhaps without their ovaries or breasts or other parts; they are a wall of fury and love and power, screaming and calling out, singing and sobbing and saying shit like *WE'VE GOT YOU* through a megaphone. The mother in the darkness picks up a flashlight and shines it around and thinks, *Yeah, time to go*, tugs on a few ropes that have been unfurled to assist her ascent and gets pulled up and out into the light into a mighty band of furious, broken, beautiful women who give the sweetest kind of comfort—which is to be a witness—after kicking serious ass and getting the mother to climb up and out. Everyone is still sad. Nothing is solved. But also, this particular mother is not screaming inconsolably in a horrible hole in the dirt, and she is not dead. *You're not alone, and you never will be.* And that is everything.

Of course, when a child dies, I think of the child, but my job now is to think of the mother when she writes to me or calls me, because we are, as mothers of children who have died, obliged to do our best to make this mother's experience in that horrible sinkhole of grief a one-off. That doesn't mean she's not still grieving, but she's in a different place now. She's in the pack that grieves up top, from a distance, but not in a distanced way.

I rarely cry when I talk about the death of my son, because I know well enough that if I let myself drop, I might keep dropping, and I want to be in the world, however problematic and confusing and heartbreaking the world might be. The Loss Ladies get it, whether they were in our group for three hours or three years. I know I could call any one of them at any time and, without even identifying myself, scream into the phone without judgment, and they could do the same with me. Although our stories were intensely sad, the experience we had being together and creating together was a living, textured kind of happiness, a happiness with blood in it, a happiness like stepping into the healing dark and finding someone to greet you there, holding a lamp and saying, *This way, the worst has passed.*

Happiness, like grief, can feel ruthless, but I have found a happiness in writing that allows the grief to live there too, as one cannot be known and understood without the knowledge and understanding of the other.

Happiness, like the love I bear for these women, can also be a magical, pure emotion that children feel most acutely of all, and yet another reason why their pain disproves the suffering-to-salvation equation. I cry when I see another mom down there in the hole of the world, and all I can do is scream and sob and wait. It's the part of my life I take seriously, my most important side gig—to be full of rage and aching, and to show up and keep watch with all the others. I cry a lot, in fact, because children die and mothers suffer, but unless you love me or loved my child, you'll never see it. The price of that truth is too dear.

The Loss Ladies met for three years once a month on Zoom, and our group included poets, physicians, social workers, nonprofit executives, health care workers, full-time mothers, ministers, musicians, lawyers, visual artists, teachers, and mental health advocates—every race, creed, and sexuality. The Angel of Death does not discriminate. For three years, we discussed written work and supported one another in the writing of grief and generating art in community; people came and went or joined when they could. After the worst of the pandemic had passed in 2022, some of us met in Maui, where we kayaked, did goat yoga, ate delicious meals, and did more of the same writing and wailing and working at the stunning oceanside home of one of our members.

Our WhatsApp group chat was as funny as it was profound. In it, we shared resources, support, and stories, and we started an alternative milestones tradition during which we remembered every dead child's birthday and death date. We talked about how to parent our children after death. In rewriting these narratives of grief, I came to understand how grief can act as a divination of love, love that is an inexhaustible resource—transformative because it is immortal. Community creates a container of mutual support and asks questions that have no answers but are important to ask regardless. Can we love beyond the grave? Can we meet each other in those liminal spaces, whatever and wherever they might be? Through story, we can bear wounds that will never heal, and we can connect with people who have been forced to do the same. We do not have to feel—or be—alone.

After three years, I stopped the formal meetings of the Loss Ladies group—although I still miss them—when I realized that I needed to attend to my own emotional limits, which had been stretched too much and for too long. That's the other thing about teaching and holding space for others' stories: You must know when you need to pull your energy back inside and focus on the narratives of your own life. Women aren't trained to do this, so most of us suck at it.

In *The Grieving Brain*, Mary-Frances O'Connor, a pioneer in the study of the neurology of grief, maps what I'd call "the brain on grief" using functional MRI scans and other empirical data to approach the emotional experience from a scientific perspective. Essentially, these scans show that when you grieve, your brain is actively trying to solve a puzzle that cannot be solved. Where has the person gone when they were just here? Something is off, the brain senses, but how to fix it? The synapses fire, but to what end? Writing is a lot about solving puzzles: What metaphor to place here? What is the character doing there? Is this the time for a drum solo or a guitar riff? What is the narrator feeling in their body during a scene or inside an intense emotional moment?

I've written a lot about grief, and this book is particularly dedicated to those who are doing that work—the how and the why, and several potential ways in and through. As O'Connor illustrates and as others have noted, the death of a loved one is the ultimate human experience—a reckoning with identity in every sense of the word. You're a mother or a spouse or a lover or a sister or an aunt . . . and then you're not. Rug pulled, or more accurately, ripped out, from beneath you. It's lonely and sad and alienating, like a Kafkaesque lunar landscape in which you wake to find that you are not only a bug, but everything is covered in superglue and there are no lights anywhere. You're stuck, you're alone, you're sitting in the dark, and you're a roach with a sad human mind and everything you touch sticks to you. What do you do? Grief is, in this sense, the most original articulation of human experience. That interior landscape can be treacherous, yes, but it's also a source of healing. I've often been asked, "Are you ever going to stop writing about your son?" As if that part of my heart is done telling stories or feeling things. The answer is: Never. (The *fuck off* is silent but implied.)

My brain and my heart and my typing fingers will *never* stop making meaning of Ronan's life and death. And anyone who doesn't understand that and wishes on any level that I would stop—or that *any* mother would stop—has no business being anywhere in my energetic field. Boundary erected and fortified. Case closed. *Ba-bump.*

Once you've known deep grief, you quickly find others who have known it too. When my daughter was born with red hair, I suddenly saw little gingers everywhere when I hadn't noticed as many before, even though I, too, am a redhead. That fierce light born of grief, hard-won, attracts the same fierce light. In the artists' community at Yaddo, I was introduced to the powerful work of graphic novelist and visual artist Leela Corman, whose work addresses PTSD, losing her first daughter suddenly, plus the inherited trauma of the Holocaust in Poland and Ukraine, during which many of her family members perished.

Of course, I knew none of this when I visited Leela's

studio, which is one of the singular joys, for me, of being at an arts community with visual artists: their work is so tactile, so materials-based, so tangible and three-dimensional. The materiality of language has a texture the way art and music do, but visual artists and musicians get to move around more and make more noise.

This is especially thrilling for someone like me, whose drawing ability halted at age three with the stick figure. One wall of Leela's studio was lined (I mean, perfectly lined) with note cards, and sitting on an easel were frames for her latest graphic novel. I was drawn to her and to her work in a way that felt elemental, necessary, and then I looked at the pages of the 2015 graphic piece she'd written about her daughter: "PTSD: The Wound That Never Heals." The paintings move from scenes of daily life with soft edges and colors to terrifying and shape-focused to dreamlike.

I marched up to Leela with my plastic cup of wine and said, "I want to be your friend." I did not ask for an audition, I went straight for the role. A sad mother heart knows another as she knows her own—imperfectly but intuitively, the deepest kind of knowing. I read Leela's graphic essay many times during that Yaddo stay, and I sent it to every close friend of mine, saying, "This is the picture of the narrative agony I was trying to set down in my work." Leela talks about how for the longest time after her daughter died, she pushed herself: physically, creatively, artistically. Then, one day, she simply stopped and was still. She rested for a long, long time, and it was only then that she could write about the grief experience. In an interview, she noted that "eventually, very gentle yoga, gentler than I'd ever given myself permission to do before, helped me get to a base level of functioning." Her personal recovery was related to the making of art, but it wasn't forceful or about pushing through; it was about lying still in the middle of the painful experience, watching what appeared in the tornado that had been thrust upon her life, and sitting with it, clear-eyed, not knowing what would appear, but surrendering to whatever emerged.

Grief stories can feel like they're rocketing through a bullhorn, but we can tell them differently if they're told from a place of stillness, which is a kind of embodied trust. Or, as Colin Bedell, a.k.a. QueerCosmos and everyone's favorite Instagram astrologer, reminds us, quoting Rachel Botsman, "Trust is a confident relationship with the unknown." I've got that quote on my desk too, snuggled up to Rilke, alongside a piece of paper my daughter gave to me when she was four that reads, "Ronan. Charlie. Love that will never brak," in the sweetest five-year-old misspelling of all time.

My friend, the poet Katie Ford, teaches a class called Poetry of the Unseen. Not only is Katie an extraordinary teacher with an inimitable mind, but she's been writing from another realm since I first met her and started reading her poems in 1998, while we were in divinity school together. We'd be at a friend's house baking brownies and pizza and she'd read a draft and everyone would be speechless. In this class, she talks about inspiration as "interruption," which might also be conceptualized as a kind of arrested or exquisite attention. This singularity in the line, in the metaphor, in the image acts as a bulwark against the danger of a single story. A deeply specific moment doesn't narrow your view but floods your brain with alternative narratives. In this way, craft is the ultimate, ethical, original articulation of a truth that holds within it so much of what is indescribable—what we cannot know but can only intuit through language or the reach toward language or feel as sensations in our bodies. Or, as Katie said, "The work of the edge or liminality [in a poem] is that blurred boundaries convey an endlessness as well as a division." This threshold or thinning happens between the creator and the work itself, but it also happens to the reader, to the viewer. The bloom of insight and inspiration can be quiet, subtle, but with dramatic results. A thing described so intently and specifically, so within a descriptive or metaphorical boundary, can make the sky around it seem bigger than it's ever been, perhaps even limitless. In writing courses, we call it going from the particular to the universal. I might be the only woman alive who as a ten-year-old girl with a wooden leg was shoveling heaps of snow and stacking chopped wood for the winter. Yet most people have had some experience with tedious, hard work not of their own choosing, often in childhood.

Once, in our Zoom gathering, one of the Loss Ladies read an essay that knocked my heart out of my chest and sent it beating madly around the room like a fiery, unstoppable thing. I can still remember sitting on the bed, in the sun, sweating but cold at the same time. My entire body was covered in goose bumps, and my cheeks were burning. I was speechless with awe and sadness and rage at her loss, and respect for her decision to write down what felt unspeakable. I felt ferocious and grateful. We were all silent, staring into the little dot cameras of our computers. I didn't know what to say, but all I could think was this: Her act of telling that story, to us, in that moment, had flooded my whole being with light. The world was new, the world was terrible, the world was full of love so strong it could break your heart, over and over again. All those things were true, all at the same time.

Share it to bear it. Truly. Katie Ford again, talking about the mystery of a poem's power:

> Poems are unfinished by the poet—or should be thought of as such—and await a reader's interpretive creativity, which is a "making" of its own kind. The reader finishes the poem. The poem is not complete until it is received by another. It lies dormant as an offering until that moment, perhaps like holy water in a basin that is always in waiting. Perhaps. And what does the water know of what it will next be used for, what hand will touch it? What might it bless or bury? In the same way, the author is protected from ever knowing what might be made of her work by individual readers. This is a very crucial secret, and highly intimate.

Reading and writing are both forms of deep and profound emotional and intellectual intimacy. When we work through an experience via the making of art, it becomes an offering—to the reader, to the viewer, to the listener, to the world. Now we know what someone has chosen to tell or show us about their story: the grappling and struggling and triumph. Their story becomes part of ours, and that cannot be undone. We are connected by writing and thinking and talking about this universal experience of loss.

In *The Observable Universe*, writer and visual artist Heather McCalden writes, "Words are how we know something happened. We say what we saw and the experience appears. It becomes observable." The story has been told, and now its existence is undeniable—it shines. A light is a light. In the most miserable crucibles and in the darkest spaces, one light attracts another, joins another, until that space is lit up, stitched together as if by lightning, and at the end of each bolt is a person—one of Rumi's night travelers, full of light—sharing a story in order to bear that story, no matter how terrible or true. Just as we're meant to be storytellers, we're also meant to tell our stories to each other. Nobody was meant to bear these stories alone. And when we tell these stories, travel with them, we bear that light, share it, guard it, evoke it, keep and guard it like the treasure that it is.

– 4 –

Horizons of Meaning

THE ETHICS OF EMPATHY

In fact history does not belong to us; we belong to it.
—Hans-Georg Gadamer,
from *Truth and Method*
(*Wahrheit und Methode*)

It's a hot and humid summer in the late 1980s, and we're searching for my grandmother's grave. Once a year, we return to my parents' hometown, a small rural community of eight hundred people in Illinois three hours south of Chicago, where you are either "on the farm" or "living in town" after retiring and selling the farm or passing it on to your kids. The landscape, the culture, the people: it was the Heartland and the Bible Belt combined. During the summer, we work on my great-uncle's pig farm, where he also grows corn and beans. The work is hot and gross: early to rise, early to bed.

My mom is driving someone's old Cadillac with no air-conditioning, so the windows are open to the sounds and smells of a rural midsummer: cow shit baking in the heat, air that feels thick enough to slice with your hand, and a constant thrum of unseen bugs. I'm sweating in long pants because if I wear shorts that reveal my artificial leg, people in this town literally stop to gawk at me as if I have absconded from a zoo or a freak show, with an alarming look in their eyes that says, *I'll take this one to the revival tent and get her healed up by the Lord.* After taking a turn down one road (they all look the same to me—a giant grid of straight roads and farmhouses evenly spaced out, like a living Monopoly board), my mom stops and says, "Wait, this is wrong." She turns around, tries another road, and again understands this isn't the right way, although it's clear she doesn't know how to correct her mistake. We drive for hours, my mom growing increasingly panicked, as if failing to find her mother's grave will feel like losing her mother all over again. "I thought I would remember where to go by keeping my eye fixed to the horizon," Mom says, but as the afternoon light thickens, the horizon looks the same in every direction: sky lowering into the earth and the earth rising into the sky, as if they could merge. In that moment in the car, we are living in two different realms or qualities of time: my mom's faulty memory of the grave, and the time, when she was twenty-three, just after her mom died at fifty-seven after a lifetime of heart issues caused by a childhood case of scarlet fever.

"When my mom died, I sat on the couch for almost three days," my mom says. She rarely talks about her mom, but her obvious distress is making her chatty. "I stared at the curtains on the windows that your dad and I had just put up. I hated them. I hated them so much that all I could think about was how ugly they were and how much I wanted to rip them down."

"Did you?" I ask, struggling to imagine my petite mom, a tidy and relentless housekeeper, ripping down curtains.

"I didn't." She peers through the windshield as if getting closer to the warm glass will help. "All the roads are melting together." It sounds like she's about to cry, which horrifies me because I am fourteen and still don't fully understand that my mom is a person separate from me, someone who had a life before I was born or might have a single thought ever that is not about or connected to me. I know my parents have known each other their entire lives, and that they were with my grandmother when she died a few months after they were married. I'm a teenager, and a stereotypically sullen and myopic one, so all I can think to say is "Oh."

Today, I recognize that nothing was wrong with her curtains. She and my father lived with them for years. The point was that she wanted to rage and cause some destruction. But in the rural Illinois of 1967, nice young women didn't cause damage.

In the heat of that borrowed Cadillac, my mom continues. "What I wish is that I'd spent more time on that couch, hating those curtains. I got up too soon. Nobody understood the idea of grieving then. You were just supposed to get on with it." I also don't understand the idea of grieving, but I had been sent to therapy when I was six because I was convinced my mom was going to die and threw a massive fit every time she left the house. So that bit I get.

"Maybe we should get new curtains at home," I offer. "You can rip down the old ones." The image of my well-mannered mom ripping through our heavy eighties-era floral curtains puts me on the edge of a giggle.

"Oh, well, I don't know," my mom says, laughing through what sounds like the beginning of tears. "Maybe. But first let's go get some pie in town. It's getting dark."

We never found my grandmother's grave. It's somewhere on the windswept hazy, windswept plain of rural Illinois, where dreams go to die a strangled, slow death framed by heavy brocade.

•

Our memories are oriented by and rooted in truth; they are also fluid, changing over time, and therefore not reliable as evidence of an *absolute* truth. We may feel hemmed in by our horizons, or oriented somehow, but in truth, we are unreliable eyewitnesses to the events of our own lives. In the witness box, our testimony would be easily unraveled according to legal standards. Memories are rock solid and also ultimately deniable; they direct our stories, and they are also directionless. This doesn't make them—or us—wrong. In fact, it makes us human.

In this context, personal narratives or memoir naturally lead to essential questions that are important to consider as a writer and a reader: First, if memory is so wack-a-doo, how can we write stories that adhere, even in part, to some truth, given that telling the truth is a prerequisite for nonfiction?

Second, why should we read or care about the real lives of people we don't know?

Behold! There's a twentieth-century German philosopher who thought about this very thing, or at the very least, I have relied on my interpretation of his systems of interpretive thought to talk about this very thing. Hans-Georg Gadamer, or HGG, as I call him when I discuss his theories in class, had ideas that can help us draw a fundamental distinction between empathy and sympathy in narrative, particularly in memoir, which is an essential part of what we do. That's not what he set out to do, of course, but I think my pivot would thrill him.

I was introduced to the work of HGG by Professor Francis Schüssler Fiorenza at Harvard Divinity School, who taught hermeneutics in the big lecture hall twice a week very early in the morning. I think he said "in other words" at least a hundred times in each lecture; philosophy is a tricky thing and often needs to be approached from many angles. The term *hermeneutic*, according to folk etymology, is in honor of Hermes, Greek messenger of the gods, who invented language and writing, and the figure who is routinely blamed for logistical mishaps during any Mercury retrograde. Hermeneutics is an analysis of our approaches to and relation of what we deem to be true about a thing or situation (a piece of art or music, a time in history, a biblical or legal text, a memory of driving with your mother, etc.).

Like Nietzsche, HGG adopts the notion that all human understanding includes a perspective, a situatedness or positionality that cannot be avoided or discounted (essentially, all the biographical details that make you uniquely you). Nobody can utter a positionless, absolute truth that can be applied to all people across time and history. HGG would have been all over TikTok and Instagram, which are positionality and particularity writ large and in moving color. Everyone can have an opinion, an idea, an experience, shared or otherwise, but nobody can claim that there is ONE right way to do or be or think. To even say one is right or wrong in terms of expression and art-making would throw our stoic German intellectual into a full-on tizzy.

In his epic and very long work *Truth and Method*, which was basically the *Da Vinci Code*–esque bestseller of philosophy tomes among mid-twentieth-century white dude philosophers and academics, HGG sets forth four concepts that are essential to his hermeneutics: prejudice, tradition, authority, and horizon. Horizon is the one we're most interested in here as it relates to writing and narrative and the ethics of creation, but let's look at the other three briefly, because like any good philosophical system, they're all connected. Also, every philosophical system at this time was like a pile of tangled jewelry; you tug on one necklace and the whole jewelry box comes with it.

For HGG, *prejudice* means a prejudgment, which includes any assumptions that are part of making a claim that something is true or knowable in a particular way. Consider something as simple as *Rocks don't move, they lie on the ground until moved by a person, an animal, a storm with strong wind*, or even something more complicated like *Democracy is the best and most equitable system of government.*

Neither of these statements is necessarily more solid or true or evidentiary than the other: they're simply expressions of belief. When we express a belief, we (and others) exercise our understanding to either affirm or reject it. Unlike our modern interpretation of the word, HGG's *prejudice* is not necessarily a damning categorization (see the rocks example above), but simply empirical information predicated on sensory, emotional, and intellectual observation. Or grist for the mill, as the saying goes, with your mind being the mill.

The way HGG uses *prejudice* is, in fact, neutral: it undeniably exists, and we use our brains and methods of understanding (all of which are open to interrogation) to decide what is true or not true, to decide which beliefs to accept and which ones to challenge, to accept or reject a way of life or a way of being. In other words, each prejudice is an opportunity to exercise agency—to make a decision. Our forejudgments, or prejudices, according to HGG, allow us to access the knowledge we must marshal in order to make decisions in the first place; this includes language, which by its variant, interpretive, and flexible nature must also include doubt to include certainty. You can't have one without the other.

The word *tradition* is also used expansively. HGG believed that we cannot escape our traditions or prejudices (or, as we might understand it, our lens of experience through which we allocate meaning to the events of our lives). How often have you looked at a picture of a long-dead relative and thought, *Ohhh shit, there I am*? Genetics cannot be outrun, and they can be deeply unfair. However, just because we share a nose shape or body type with an ancestor doesn't mean we're stuck believing in our grandparents' racist ideologies or our parents' weird religious practices; in fact, HGG's whole notion of prejudice is founded on a requirement for wiggle room, or an opportunity to change our minds or beliefs—to *pivot*, as we might say now. For HGG, the door to change is always propped open on a single hinge, swinging this way and that, up and down and all around, a big swirly door in a wild wind. In fact, prejudice and tradition, in HGG's system of thought, create the very conditions of our knowledge, which is neutral in the sense that it creates the launching pad for any meaningful inquiry without saying the launching pad is rotten or inviolate from the get-go. Useful, of course, when writing about one's life. You can't pick your pad or your parents. But you do have choices about what you do or think next.

Tradition, then, creates the conflict that fuels the quest, and all narratives are, in fact, a kind of quest. A questing character is a questioning, evolving character willing to be forged in the fire of their experiences, and it's also a character a reader invests in and stays interested in. You can't get unstuck if you don't know the texture of what you're stuck in (a thick bog, a shitty relationship, bad traffic). Tradition can only be claimed *if you alter it*—it's never the same as any that came before, precisely because it has been filtered through your unique lens (prejudices) by the process of thinking itself. Borrowing in part from Hegel, HGG's worldview posits that tradition *provokes* rather than affirms the status quo (which might easily tip into tyranny), because it sheds light on our prejudgments and forces us to try to understand or reconcile our new belief with our old, inherited one that is made new ("taken up" or vacuumed up) by this process of examination, which in turn makes a tradition new and unique to us because we are both critical and creative in how we approach and then apply it. We scoop it up and make it new; it's like cleaning the litter box of the mind, which doesn't happen just once, but over and over again.

HGG's understanding of authority was also dependent on and linked with the act of deep reflection, itself a moral imperative. Memorization of a text or rote belief in a system constitutes not authoritative expressions but tyrannical ones (which would include all strict orthodoxies). To understand, we must examine, which is to say critique, rather than parrot what we've been told to believe because it's the way it is or was or should be. In that sense, our understanding is rooted in our histories, personal and collected, or what HGG calls "historically effected/effective consciousness." Your situation or positionality is not restrictive in a negative sense; the limits of your life are, in fact, what allow you to open to the process of creating something new, because you must activate your understanding to fully know them in the first place. This system gives us the ethical mandate to try to respect and make room for everything in the world, including all the people—and stories—within it.

Finally, we get to the phenomenological horizon and the "fusion of horizons," which is the last step in this long process of interpreting and interacting with the world around us (and behind and in front of us—read on). HGG believed that each person has a horizon that is limited due to the perspectival nature of knowing (i.e., you can't know what you don't know). Just as a literal horizon shows us the line between heaven and earth, the epistemic or known horizon within each person makes true knowledge possible, understanding that knowledge is never fixed, but always preparing to fuse with new understanding—note the word *fuse*, not *burn down*, *eliminate*, *destroy*, *silence*, *discount*, *demonize*, or *disallow*. A horizon acts as a temporal frame that includes the present moment (present culture and society and how we interact with it), the remembered past (tradition), as well as the projected future. Like a shimmering line of TV static or a machine that tracks your heartbeats, this horizon is rooted in time, and also exists outside of it; it includes your fears, your dreams, your body, how and where you grew up, your gender, and your language. Then it creates opportunities to alter these specifics of your unique positionality in space, history, and time. You belong to your history, but this can be revised; you belong to the larger history of the world, so even in your individuation, you are not off the hook for a ruthless examination of these different histories. Truth, for HGG, is an *event*, a kind of epiphany that takes place in a limited space and makes possible new spaces, which might be limitless precisely *because* each one is circumscribed by position, prejudice, tradition, and history, and each space is cast under a scrutinous eye that is also willing to see things differently. You can't take an ethical stand if you don't even know where to sit. Whitman said, "I contain multitudes," which is one way I understand HGG's horizon metaphor, but with one crucial difference: the fusion, understood as an ever-expanding, forever-evolving horizon in which we find ourselves engaged and changed. We make history and history makes us. In this way, we belong to ourselves, to one another, to our communities, and to the world. Or, as the poet Katie Ford said once in an interview, "All lives have many worlds circulating within, many ideas and decisions that cause duress, confusions, and clarities. The daily life arrives and doesn't stop arriving, while the transcendent life appears and sustains, then recedes and rests." These two zones, if you will, make of themselves a horizon.

This is not historicism, and it isn't relativism either, but a kind of middle ground or thought beam balanced between the two. The concept of horizon can only be generous and flexible *because* it is limited. There is no view from nowhere without limitation, nothing can be examined or understood. Fairness is then predicated on an acknowledgment of limitation, which in this framework is a gift, a path to empathy. A horizon makes possible vision that is both distant and near (philosophical bifocals if you will); we can see what is close-up (our stories) and what is far away (other people's stories, or history itself) without excluding or discounting either. The fusion is the integration of the individual speaker with the world wherein no part of the person is demolished; everything is preserved because it is transmuted.

The image that comes to mind is the weird dessert my mother often made for church potlucks. From a distance,

Mom's cake looks like an ordinary white cake made from a Duncan Hines mix covered in whipped cream. But then, after the first bit has been forked off, the white cake is revealed to also include small tunnels of green Jell-O that have been inserted from the top, and also, some of these strange tunnels contain parts of walnuts and maybe even a raisin. Up close and far away: very different views leading to different assumptions, same yummy cake with a green surprise inside. Go down a rabbit hole, and you might find rabbits; you also might find gold.

So, what does any of this have to do with narrative and writing? Everything, really. It's about veracity in our stories and the ethical telling of them. It's a way of understanding how we connect with or disconnect from people, and what the consequences of both might be, in our individual lives as well as across time and history. Although this is not precisely what HGG had in mind, I identify an ethics of empathy (versus sympathy, which is one-note and distancing) in HGG's fusion of horizons.

Given this limited horizon that is always open to expansion and change, given that every piece of knowledge or evidence that falls into it is absorbed, examined, and repurposed, then every story you read falls into that horizon. There's no choice, only the decision you make after a rigorous examination of the information, which involves a willingness to look deeply at the self. That person's story is part of your story now, because remember: the door never fully closes. That is, in fact, the nature of how knowledge works—we can't even really get out of it if we adhere to the core tenants of HGG's thinking. I think of the horizon in a very expansive way—as being changed with every interaction with every person or story. It is never static. It is out of time, *and* it is grounded in time. It is generous, porous, limited, and in this way, it becomes boundless in its ability to locate truth and meaning in a story that is also generous and utterly unique. I find this a beautiful distillation of the mechanics of ethical connection in story and in life. And if history is what make us, and we make history, as HGG suggests, then we need the stories of other people. Otherwise, we wouldn't be able to access thought, and without thought, we'd feel nothing—not love, not desire, not fear, not regret, not shame—nothing at all. Our horizons would be lonely and sad. We'd be flat popsicle-stick people living in a cardboard diorama.

Here's another way to say it: the more you know about someone, the less likely you are to kill them, because your horizon has fused with theirs and vice versa. Literally everyone matters in my interpretation of HGG's worldview *simply because they exist*. This doesn't mean you have to like everyone or their stories, but it does mean you cannot ignore or discount them, pretend they don't exist, or tell them that they don't matter and that they can't make art.

Within this conceptual understanding of the meaning and power of story, we are all responsible for one another. And narrative, then, especially personal narrative and intimate stories of strife and loss and the cost of love, is an act of service, to the self and to the world, as the self and the world create the horizon of existence, up close and far away.

The Zen Buddhist teacher Frank Ostaseski, in his book *The Five Invitations: What Death Can Teach Us About Living Fully*, explores these invitations: (1) Don't wait. (2) Welcome everything, push away nothing. (3) Bring your whole self to the experience. (4) Find a place of rest in the middle of things. (5) Cultivate don't know mind.

If we take these to heart, which I have, and if we think about HGG's insistence that it just *all really matters*, then how do we distinguish what it is we want to say? A common question for writers is "Why do you write?" Of course, that changes over the course of one's life, as values and beliefs shift and horizons fuse and do magical things and chaos ensues. When I first started writing, I did it because it was fun (imagine!) and I didn't like to do my chores (and still don't). In my twenties, I did it because I thought it would bring me the love of the world (whoops!) and because I thought I knew a lot of things and boy, did people need to know about them. In my thirties, I wrote because it kept me alive when my son was dying. In my forties, I write because the world is more interesting and chaotic to me than it's ever been now that I realize how little I actually know. (I really hope fifty isn't the new thirty, as I barely made it out of that decade.) The meditation teacher Jack Kornfield and others refer to the not knowing as "the beginner's mind," which is a fun place to be, because if you don't know anything for certain, you're curious about everything. Life becomes interesting and juicy then, even when and if it's challenging or unbearably sad.

Here's another idea, and one I think many have found

useful. If you're wondering about how to write your story or if you should: Look for a book you wish existed when you were going through something hard and were unable to find a source of guidance or comfort. Who will it serve? Who will pull it off the shelf with relief, anticipation, joy, and maybe even a bit of healthy dread about what might be discovered in there? Who will read it and want to stay in the world, even for one more day? Write *that* book. Then, when the book is released, detach from any feelings about its reception. Don't read what's written about you online (remember—it all lands in the horizon!). If writing is an act of service, then the only pressure you need to manage is what all creators must: the making of it to the best of your ability *in the moment*. Only then will it have possible staying power.

Who is it for, your work? (Answer: It's not just for you, and likely not for everyone.) The goal of art is not to become rich and famous, although maybe this happens for some, and if it does, it won't last forever. The goal of making art is not to try to make people love you or to affirm your essential goodness or worthiness (these tactics will fail; I've tried them). But art can spring out of loneliness and despair as a gift for someone—a light in the tunnel for someone who needs it. You might fuse a horizon with someone you will never meet or know, with someone who is long dead—what a mysterious, beautiful concept, a world stitched together with lightning bolts of ideas, constellations of truth, a bunch of horizons bouncing around, making new meaning and connection. Those are the conversations you're looking to have with the world, with yourself, with people you know and love, and with people you'll never meet. And you do it through the art you make, which itself necessitates an interplay between the conscious and the unconscious.

•

We didn't find my grandmother's gravestone on that trip, although it was there, within a few miles of us, and we were never that far away from her. When I first read HGG's theory of the fusion of horizons, I thought about that moment, and the intimacy of being disoriented by what you thought you knew, or the way you thought you should go, all while creating a new memory, a new story, but building on a preexisting memory. The fluidity of horizons and memories means stories are literally always in motion. HGG was certainly not a Buddhist, but I can't help thinking about what Tara Brach says about mindfulness meditation as a tool to help us wake up from the story of separation. In HGG's system, creating story is a kind of mindfulness in action, in which people are natural storytellers, willing truth-tellers, but nobody can claim a single, inviolate truth about experience. Nobody can claim, *This is exactly how it was*; they can only claim, *This is my memory of what it was for me.*

In the end, to rework HGG's quote about history for the writer or artist: in truth, our stories do not belong to us but rather we to them, and each of us to one another.

– 5 –

The Shadow World

WRITING THROUGH TRAUMA AND TRAGEDY

I cannot say
that I have gone to hell
for your love
but often
found myself there
in your pursuit.
—William Carlos Williams,
from "Asphodel, That Greeny Flower"

On the edge of one winter over a decade ago, I sat with my son, Ronan, on the couch as the sun set. It's strange to think of him now, gone for so much longer than he was alive, but I can vividly remember that time of my life when darkness seemed to be arriving earlier each day. In my chest, I felt a sinking weight and a slow opening in the same moment; here was such great love, matched equally by grief—such an equitable balance that it felt impossible. My heart was a flowering stone, rocklike and hard, but petaled and colorful, shedding one shape for another, each beat a sudden motion signaling the shift, jarring but tender. And then this: *Fuck you, God. I'm finished with you.* I often wondered what a broken heart looks like, how it behaves: Does it go purple with effort? Shrink like an oyster squirted with lemon before it's gobbled up? When explaining why we've made this or that decision we say, *I've had a change of heart.* In the Bible, God hardened Pharaoh's heart as well as the hearts of the Israelites (and both for plot-driven, narrative purposes). We say, *My heart goes out to you*, as if we can connect to another heart via sonar or telepathy. Heartbreak: this clutch in the chest that gapes—tenacious like faith but lacking the comfort and clarity that faith is intended to provide. What gives? These were the thoughts in my mind; even when I wasn't consciously thinking them, they were present in the quiet, in the shadows, and especially at night.

I had long ago chucked my old, personal visions of God as a man doing good things for good people, but I respect people who believe in a comforting God without empirical proof of God's existence; this is, we're told, the essence of faith, and it doesn't have to be doubtless or mindless, and it doesn't necessarily mean a passive acceptance of shitty, heart-wrenching situations. People who believe in God are not stupid, although it's often difficult to believe this, especially when people are offering provocative but lazy theological perspectives and trying to obliterate the personhood of people they've decided are bad based on stupid interpretations of biblical passages, some of which don't even exist.

Bad theology abounds, sadly, but this is (or should be) different from the thoughtful theology of people of faith.

I've never thought that faith was stupid, or the stuff of fools, or the opium of the masses. Yes, it's often presented that way in public discourse—easy solutions offered up as made-for-television answers for overwhelmingly complicated problems—but writers as smart and badass as Dostoevsky, Atwood, O'Connor (to name a few), and others, living and dead, have been concerned with faith. What is faith in anything, and how do we find and keep it? How do we hold up when it's tested? What's the point of having it in the first place? Comfort? Salvation? Unique conversational fodder for a cocktail party or perhaps a tactic to make sure nobody talks to you at that party? Which brings every theologian—and every person who lives long enough—to the point of pondering that Job-ish moment of the test, when the world goes dark and options are zero. In a word: Suffering. Evil. The unthinkable. *Where is God?* people ask in times of great distress and calamity, which is another way of asking, *Where am I? Who am I?* and *Why?*

Who could believe in a God that would allow natural disasters, from a tsunami or an earthquake to a destructive wildfire or a hurricane? The floods and the plagues and the diseases and the epidemics and the deaths from preventable illness? All the natural events that ravage and destroy? On a (literally) more molecular level, and for me, obviously, a personal one, how can a person believe in a God that would allow the existence of Tay-Sachs, a disease that would certainly be a major contender for the title of Most Evil Disease if such awards existed? The history of humanity swirls around people attempting to have faith in something, anyone and anything, in spite of but also within the faith of loss and grief. But to deconstruct faith, it's helpful to have an honest look at the content and construct and perhaps misunderstanding of evil itself. In the winter of 2013, months before my son died, I kept asking, *What is it? What is evil?* It felt like high school math class, when we'd solve some dumb algebra equation and come out with a number that made no sense to me. What did the number mean? Was it big, little, the shape of a kitten, what? Being told, *It's just the right answer* was not enough, akin to saying, *That's just how it is.* Okay, but why?

What is evil? Is it a person, a movement, the divine mastermind behind an event? What were all the wars for if not to eradicate it? What are they currently for? Evil, evil, evil. Not the sharp-toothed and mischievous red demon with ears and a tail, muscular thighs and a supercilious grin, but what? (My dad used to dress up as the devil for church Halloween parties, arguing that the best way to mess with Satan is to laugh at him. Meanwhile, I hovered over the punch bowl, horrified by the sight of my father in red tights and a leotard.)

As a subject of deep inquiry, evil is a good topic to choose as a theologian, because it's a problem that isn't going away. Evil isn't trendy. It's pervasive and odorless as lethal gas and it exists in miniscule, almost undetectable ways as well as obvious, mammoth ways: from the person who, with malicious intent, makes a snide comment to a friend or acquaintance or stranger to the serial killer who searches for his latest victim with cunning and rage. We talk about the evil that arises from climate change: floods, earthquakes, tsunamis, tornados, disease. If God is the creator of the world, what does it say about him/her/it if the world is riddled with such suffering and blight? Where is God for the suffering heart, the grieving parent, the dying soldier, the innocent civilian caught in a lethal cross fire, the refrigerated trucks of overflow corpses at the height of the COVID-19 pandemic, the person watching their house burn down? For the children whose parents are swept away in a wave of water? For the parents whose children are swept away by a flash flood? For the father whose child is trapped under rubble? For a mother whose son dies of thirst in a war zone? Where is God in these images of hell? Invoking presence through absence? Lurking outside the frame, waiting for a moral version of luminol to make him/her/it visible?

During the final months of Ronan's life, I sent a lot of emails and asked a lot of questions. I asked my beloved college professor Ed Santurri to recommend books by contemporary theologians who address the problem of God and human suffering. *The Doors of the Sea: Where Was God in the Tsunami?* by David Bentley Hart is a muscular, slightly conservative-leaning but fascinating explication of various theological interpretations of evil. Although based on the 2004 tsunami, Hart's arguments and theoretical scenarios are relevant to any catastrophic event. Hart doesn't care if he offends people (and his patriarchal vision is, at some points and for this reader, very limiting), but he's no dummy, and he uses the whole machine of his mind and all the strength of his heart to try to make sense of suffering in this world, or at least to hammer to a pulp (intellectually, that is) those who use punitive theology to explain natural disaster or disease or any other random bit of evil or hardship that befalls individuals or families or countries. There's a brain behind his babble; the book is an impassioned response to those who reacted to the 2004 tsunami in Asia with theology that Hart found wrongheaded, cruel, and morally insipid. His commentary would not generate a salacious headline that *Those people deserved it for sinning against God! See what happens when you don't believe?* might, but it's worth reading and considering. If only there were more thinkers like Hart weighing in on this issue of suffering and what it's about (so much) and what it's for (if anything).

Hart first picks apart the determinist position that casts God as little more than a clockmaker—an automaton that created the world and allows its wheels to turn round and round, wholly indifferent to any outcome or result. The God of ultimate detachment and even accidental omniscience, as you can't really be omniscient if you don't care. The problem here, argues Hart, is the presumption that God can be understood to be *like us*, and operating from this misunderstanding generates skewed expectations about what a creator does or doesn't do. Any God worth His salt (no female God for Hart, it turns out, which is annoying) wouldn't bother mucking around in the same bodily forms that His finite beings are forced to inhabit and eventually die in. An apathetic God is not an uncaring God. Apatheia, or apathy, is a kind of detachment that, far from being analogous with not caring, simply suggests that there's no reason to care. God does not have feelings. God is not emotionally reactive, Hart argues, or else God couldn't be God. But haven't we been told that God so loved the world that he sent his only son? Isn't that the ultimate expression of emotion? No, Hart argues, we're simply misunderstanding the nature of God's love, which *is* apathy. If you're going to argue for omnipotence, you can't have a depressed God feeling forlorn in heaven. In other words, God can't be the master of the universe and also be emotionally available. God is not your shrink. As Kendrick Lamar might say, God's *not like us.*

This definition of apathy is interesting, but it's a strain to match it up with disasters and wildfires and floods and hurricanes and all the unreported horrors that we never hear about.

Everyone at some point in their lives starts making odd bargains with a God they claimed not to believe in, and they start asking questions indicative of magical thinking. Why does a young woman die of cancer after being in remission, leaving behind a husband and a small child? Why does a man in his mid-thirties die of a ridiculous illness that could hardly be diagnosed, let alone cured? Interesting to note that the need to ask these questions is, according to Hart, a uniquely Christian impulse if we presuppose that at its heart, Christianity seeks justice, works for goodness, wants people to be happy, cared for, and safe. (Please note: no mention here of being rich, famous, or one with a life/body/house/spouse/job to envy according to social standards/movies/*Cosmopolitan* and *W* magazine articles or having any particular political affiliation.) This is a different view of happiness, and one that incorporates an understanding of evil without getting completely on its side. And although Hart's project is about making sense of the senseless, he does admit that "pious platitudes and words of comfort seem not only futile and banal, but almost blasphemous: metaphysical disputes come perilously close to mocking the dead. There are moments, simply said, when we probably ought not to speak. But, of course, we must speak."

Yes, we must speak. But let's not be assholes when we do.

Responses to disasters, individual or collective, according to Hart, spring less from a desire to shed moral light in a dark place, and more from the desire to reiterate one's beliefs or stories, to cast aside one's fears and sorrows. In other words, it's selfish. "God has a plan!" "You can choose to see this as the unfolding of his life." "God only gives us what we can handle." "Every cloud has a silver lining." Here is just a sampling of the gross "advice" people receive during the steely confusion of despair, none of which speaks to true suffering or anguish, and all of which makes me want to punch people. The inability to even grope for a better answer is something I cannot tolerate. Saying you don't know why or you feel sad or angry is better than saying what you could find written inside any sympathy card, or the "thoughts and prayers" that politicians pointlessly extend after the latest mass shooting. If the world is intelligently designed and governed by a hands-off God, then what gives?

Disasters big and small, private and epic, Hart asserts, teach us nothing: nothing about the world, nothing about God, nothing about our own finitude. They are simply disasters. That said, he holds forth on how mass human suffering is not understood (as in, explained) so much as touched upon in the texts of the Judeo-Christian tradition. He also makes clear the difference between extracting meaning and making sense of a situation. If that doesn't make sense, read on. And he intends *meaning* with a small *m*, not some existential curtain that can be brought down on the whole world order, condemning it to hell (which is covered in another part of the book).

Hart believes that people who say, *See? See? How could the God you believe in be a good God if he allows* that? are exposing a failure of understanding and belief:

> It seems a curious delusion—but apparently it is one shared by a great number of the more passionate secularists—to imagine that Christianity has never at any point during the two millennia of its intellectual tradition considered the problem of evil, or confronted the reality of suffering and death, or at any rate responded to these things with any subtlety: that Christians have down through the centuries simply failed to notice every single instance of flood, earthquake, or tempest, pestilence, famine, or fire, war, genocide, or slaughter; or that every Christian who has been crippled, or has contracted a terminal illness, or has watched his wife die of cancer, or has stood at the graveside of his child has somehow remained inexplicably insensible to the depths of his own pain and to the dark moral and metaphysical enigmas haunting every moment of his grief.

Good point. The main problem is that this kind of blame-thinking posits God incorrectly as "a finite ethical agent." This isn't logically sound, Hart argues. You can't view God as omnipotent and all-powerful and then expect God to "agree" to arrange your life in a happily ordered way that is to your liking. God can't be your life coach or party planner or ever-wise matchmaker. In other words, God doesn't swipe left or right—you're on your own. An omnipotent, from-the-beginning God cannot adapt his "make people happy" strategies for each new decade or century. A farmer in the fifteenth century wanted something different than the modern CEO living in a city of millions of people. God doesn't change. Otherwise, God can't be God. Thus, the emotionless nature of God's love. God is infinite, the end and the beginning of all, and "unless indeed one can fathom *infinite* wisdom, one can draw no conclusions from finite experience regarding the coincidence in God of omnipotence and perfect goodness. One may still hate God for worldly suffering, if one chooses, or deny him, but one cannot in this way 'disprove' him."

It's tempting, Hart agrees, to ignore those that claim God's nonexistence by using material proof of disasters, cancers, murders, etc., but according to Hart, arguments that at first glance seem atheist are unmasked to reveal something far more interesting. For example, the presumption that the world should be just and good, which, again, is a notion (Hart claims) that is deeply rooted in the Judeo-Christian tradition:

> At the heart of all such unbelief lies an undoubtedly authentic moral horror before the sheer extravagance of worldly misery, a kind of rage for justice, a refusal of easy comfort, and an unwillingness to be reconciled to evil that no one who believes this to be a fallen world should want to disparage. For the secret irony pervading these arguments is that they would never have occurred to consciences that had not in some profound way been shaped by the moral universe of a Christian culture.

Our moral universe certainly seems depraved these days, but I think Hart is onto something. When Ronan was alive, was my raging at God over my son's condition proof that God actually existed, because my questioning presupposed that there *should* be some sort of larger goodness at work, or some force of goodness that I could conceive of, and how could I have imagined God in the first place if God didn't exist? Was that Descartes? (Turns out it was.) I studied Saint Anselm in college, and I vaguely remembered the smooth black cover of the book with the author's name written in a blue cursive scroll as if it had been engraved there like a V. C. Andrews novel, but I couldn't remember the details of his ontological argument, through which he hoped to prove the existence of God. When I asked Ed Santurri about this, he offered:

> On Anselm's ontological argument, I would say the argument is one has not properly understood

> the concept of God if one denies God's existence. By definition God is a being greater than which none can be conceived. A being who has necessary existence is greater than a being who exists just contingently or not at all.

So, if you deny God's existence, you are contradicting yourself since a being that didn't exist or might not exist is not a being "greater than which none can be conceived." A being greater than which none can be conceived must exist necessarily; otherwise, you aren't talking about the greatest conceivable. God has to be the GOAT, or nothing at all. A being greater than which none can be conceived is—by definition—one that must exist necessarily (and not contingently or simply in the mind). Ergo, God exists. This is commonly regarded as the strongest version of Anselm's ontological argument. The term *ontological argument* is Kant's phrase in referring to a variation on Anselm's argument. But subsequent commentators use the phrase *ontological argument* to designate any versions of Anselm's argument that move *a priori* from the concept or meaning of God to an affirmation of God's existence.

Hmmm . . . So God cannot be blamed for disaster and can also be transcendent. We can't be pissed off at God, as I have been, as many of us have been, even if we don't believe in God, and then claim that God doesn't exist. (Uh-oh.) God's sheer unknowability (which, again, is what makes God God in Hart's framework) means that we cannot expect God to move in ways we humans have determined, according to our own categories, as moral or good. In other words, God doesn't make moral or immoral choices, because God isn't in the business of making any choices at all, as God is beyond categories that we could imagine. (Remember, it was a bunch of robed and sandaled dudes in Nicaea, not God, who in the year 325 decided on the triune God, the categories of the Father, the Son, and the Holy Spirit, just as the whole idea of Christianity was becoming popular and accepted.) I like this reasoning because it wipes away the "I prayed and God saved me" logic that people so often believe in after they've experienced a narrow escape from some tragedy or disease. Sorry, folks, Hart posits, but God isn't up there, waiting to hear your pleas for help in a storm. God isn't up anywhere; God is God. The rest of what happens to you is chance, but that doesn't mean the world is without mystery—or, and most importantly from Hart's perspective—without moments of grace.

Just as it is troubling to point at a dying baby or a natural disaster or the photos of the young victims of a school shooting or images of war and say, *God doesn't exist if God allows this*, it is equally troubling to say that a dying baby or a murdered child or a flood-wiped community or a world ravaged by a virus has some kind of purpose in God's grand scheme of things. Again, Hart criticizes such an "odd, bland metaphysical optimism" of the notion that everything has a purpose, all events have a reason. I'm reminded of people who have suggested to me that it's too bad I didn't give *The Secret* a closer read when I was pregnant, as if the Tay-Sachs gene would have just hopped right off of Ronan's

DNA strand, and mine. Or others who recommended an examination of my chakras, which must have been out of whack if such suffering had befallen me. These concepts, or what Hart would call "post-theist" views, aren't even properly atheist, because they presume that things can be put right, made new, returned to wholeness, and that Christianity, in its best modulations, is a quest for wholeness, the longing for a reconciled world, an ardent desire to mend some breach that has been created by humankind's inability not to sin. In an "elliptical way," as Hart would say, the proud atheist honors the Christian God:

> It is Christianity that not only proclaimed a God of infinite goodness but equated that goodness with infinite love. The atheist who argues from worldly suffering, even crudely, against belief in a God both benevolent and omnipotent is still someone whose moral expectations of God—and moral disappointments—have been shaped at the deepest level by the language of Christian faith.

Hart criticizes all preachers, from so-called fundamentalists to Calvin ministers, who would claim that disasters can be understood as instruments of God's will. These pundits are, he says, guilty of a "noxious pathology" and "sadistic bellowing." Hart knows how to fling a brainy insult.

Can goodness come out of bad situations? Of course, says Hart; that's the function of grace, but this idea that there is a "single will working all things," including finite things, is absurd, according to Hart, and reeks of a simple-minded determinism he finds morally and intellectually offensive, even repulsive, making God into just will, into "brute event." He goes on:

> If it gives us comfort to believe that the death of an infant from disease and the death of a serial murderer late in life from a heart attack, congenital madness and innate genius, the long fortunate life of one of nature's Romans and the brief miserable life of a born pauper are all determined by a precise calculation of what each and every one of us deserves, then it is a comfort sustained by absurdity.

Hart backs up this thinking with textual proof from the Bible, citing passages from Luke and Matthew where Jesus tells the disciples that there exists no "secret due proportion between misfortune and culpability," and, also, that a righteous man who labors all day will get no more wages than a righteous man who labors for five minutes, a parable that basically sums up this truth about life: that it isn't fair.

So, no divine calculus. No way to fully balance the scales. It is impossible to say that the death of a child or any other instance of heartbreak or event we might describe as unbearable is an "expression of divine justice." A blindly benevolent God does not dole out cures and good wishes or answer petitions like a magical wizard behind a curtain. God is not Zeus-like, flinging down thunderbolts from the sky at those who have offended him, exacting damages from their lives via natural disasters or other calamities. According to Hart, the world that Jesus was trying to usher in was one in which suffering was pointless, meaningless, and purposeless, and he suffered in an effort to bring about the end of it. A world where life finally would be fair and suffering would be eradicated. But it isn't yet; in the meantime, people suffer. What to do?

Everyone wants to be transformed by suffering, because everyone wants to be transformed into something they're not yet but might be in the future. One afternoon on the *Moon Minute* program on local Santa Fe radio ten years ago, I heard a woman discussing the different "moon stages" and the ways in which people were shedding previous habits and ways of being, trying to disrupt particular "behavioral trajectories" and break free into orbits of their own making. We want to think of suffering as something to muscle through, and we want there to be a light, some good thing at the end of the dark tunnel: a career advancement, a prize, love, recognition, a piece of pizza, a kitten, whatever. We say to one another, "You deserve this" and "You deserve that." Nobody wants to hear that we don't deserve anything at all, not really, and that part of being an adult—and an artist of any kind—is understanding that life is, like those laborers' wages in the biblical parable, radically unfair. Sadly, many people never learn this lesson, which is why it often seems like the world is full of adults acting horribly. But if we look closely enough, there we are. As Dostoevsky wrote in *The Brothers Karamazov*, "As a general rule, people, even the wicked, are much more naïve and simple-hearted than we suppose. And we ourselves are, too."

So, if God cannot be all-knowing and transcendent—which Hart ardently believes—and also spend time rolling dice across the board game of life or answering prayers like a genie responding to a rubbed lamp and deciding which wish to grant, what does God do? God just exists being God, pretty much, or at least according to Hart. God is so immense, so unfathomable, that we cannot know why things happen the way they do. We can postulate and pray and weep and gnash our teeth and go to talk therapy and drown our wonderings and sorrows in buckets of whiskey, but it doesn't change the fact that nobody knows. The phrase "things happen for a reason" feels full of the same ego with which I once flung myself into the world, believing that I (little me, all on my own) could change it. Nothing happens for a reason. Things just happen, bad things, in both invisible and calculable ways. In Hart's estimation, "the human propensity for malice should be no less a scandal to the conscience of the metaphysical optimist than the most violent convulsions of the physical world." Further, "Unde hoc malum—Whence this evil? And what sort of God permits it?"

It is Ivan Karamazov, Dostoevsky's reluctant hero, who asks this question. Our human, finite, limited minds, "bound to the conditions of time and space," cannot unravel the absurd brutality of the suffering of children; this is Ivan's reason for rejecting creation. It is an abomination of moral integrity, he argues, to say that the final healing of the world—God's eternal salvation at work, making all things new, the whole point of redemption—would somehow make sense of the suffering of innocents. They will be saved, he's told, but Ivan rejects "anything that would involve such a rescue—anything that would make the suffering of children meaningful or necessary." He rejects this price for salvation. A harmony where the suffering makes sense and is made to fit the equation is an eschatological vision he wants no part in. A world made new and whole in some promised salvific future "is not worth the tears of that one tortured child." The price of one suffering creature is too high. Ivan's rejection of God (brilliantly recounted by Hart) is "a grim, unremitting, remorseless recitation of stories about the torture and murder of (principally) children." These were true stories Dostoevsky unearthed in the press and through other sources, his own version of *Law & Order*'s famous ethos, promising grisly stories that are "ripped from the headlines." Per Hart:

> Ivan's ability to imagine a genuinely moral revolt against God's creative and redemptive order has a kind of nocturnal grandeur about it, a Promethean or Romantic or Gnostic audacity that dares to imagine some spark dwelling in the human soul that is higher and purer than the God who governs this world; and, in that very way, his argument carries within itself an echo of the gospel's vertiginous annunciation of our freedom from the "elements" of the world and from the power of the law.

It is faith that saves us, and according to Ivan's understanding, Christ was the ultimate rebel, mucking up the old world order and claiming that everyone had a place in the new one he was charged with ushering in. Instead of an atheist, a philosophical Christian? Maybe.

Part of the problem, according to Hart, is that in our advanced world, we believe we can outsmart nature, and outsmarting it is certainly encouraged. We applaud advances in treatments for medical conditions, steps toward a cure for various cancers and other potentially terminal illnesses. Each of these things is positive, of course, but each creates within us distinct illusions. Maybe that's why we seem so inordinately shocked when nature gets the better of us, because "we are free to sentimentalize or romanticize it, or even weave a veil of empty and unthreatening sanctity around it—until the moment when disease, age, infirmity, or random violence suddenly defeats us, or fire, flood, tempest, volcanic eruption, or earthquake surprises us by vaulting past our defenses." Nature becomes, in these cases, "sheer fact." We like to enjoy nature, get into the woods, experience it—we don't like to think we'll be victims of its brutal economy of life and death. The idea that *tragedy strikes* is designed to be a gripping headline, but such a statement makes it sound as if it's a rare thing, this strike. This, in turn, speaks to our expectations that avoiding calamity is possible, and this is a uniquely modern assumption. Why do we constantly say that people are *robbed* of life when they die young, that it's such a *waste*? Why can't they just be what they were, and not what they might have been?

Natural theology (looking at the world to find God), does not prove or disprove the existence of God, and does little to advance our understanding of evil. "What sort of craftsman, after all, do the internal mechanisms of nature declare?" Certainly beauty, splendor, a kind of transcendent peace, but "at the same time, all the splendid loveliness of the natural world is everywhere attended—and, indeed, preserved—by death." I loved the huge beetles that waddled bravely across the arroyo path near my house in New Mexico, their smooth black bodies rocking back and forth, looking purposeful and eager. I also saw those same beetles on their backs, dead, being hustled away by a party of ants to their huge anthill near the crosswalk. The God of natural theology is a creator and a destroyer. The face of God is visible in war as well as in a flower. People don't want to hear this, Hart points out, but there it is.

That said, the suffering and death that stem from war, according to Hart's vision of Christianity, lack any ultimate value or spiritual meaning. Instead, they are part of the shadow world, where evil is a scandal and an offense, and equally so the suffering of children. To say otherwise is to have a banal confidence in that kind of theodicy that Hart so abhors.

So, if God doesn't make choices as he is not subject to the same laws that govern human choice—namely, that one course of action cancels out the possibility of another, which is, in fact, the very nature of making a choice—then what is God doing? Well, Hart reiterates, God is being goodness in the fullest, most terrifying sense: goodness that holds everything within itself without judgment or care. God's will is not governed by anything other than his own infinite goodness;

it is not directive, it does not choose—either to grant wishes (prayers) or to subject people to Job-ish trials and calamities.

Here's the reason that God can't be evil, Hart argues: if evil is born in the will, and God has no will but the fulfillment of God's will, then he cannot have created evil, which is, in fact, understood by Christianity as a privation of the good. A lack, an "ontological wasting disease." This reminded me of Tay-Sachs, the slow fade it exacts in children—evil if anything is. Paul Tillich, a process theologian from the mid-twentieth century, removed any discussion about the willfulness of God by equating God with being itself. Literally: "The being of God is being-itself. The being of God cannot be understood as the existence of a being alongside others or above others. If God is a being, he is subject to the categories of finitude, especially to space and substance." This is a precursor to what everyone now refers to as "the universe," and the gifts it apparently gives in a benevolent way that also has no agenda and remains neutral, which is an idea I still find confusing and a bit too easy.

But here's a question: If my son lacked the cognitive refinement to understand that he had a will at all, let alone that he might choose to exercise it, then does it follow that he never knew or understood evil? If evil is a turning away from God, a turning away from light and into the privation of nothingness, of nonbeing, then was Ronan just exempt from all this thinking? Tay-Sachs is an instrument, in my mind, of evil. It destroys, eats away, and from the moment a child is born with it, they are in fact being forced back into that state of nothingness that Hart describes. In a word:

death. But Ronan was not the condition of his disease; he was not just Tay-Sachs. He was a full human being who was sick with a fatal illness that destroyed his brain and his body. Was he a victim? Certainly. But was he victimized? Not really. It's confusing. Where is God in Tay-Sachs? He's there, Hart would say, but there's no way to quantify it, understand it, or make sense of it. Enter faith.

Much of Christian thinking is predicated on a fixed God and a fixed salvation, so Hart's thinking has very real limitations for those, like me, who are not practicing members of a church; but it's refreshing to see a devout, conservative Christian lay out these theological precepts and (mis)understandings in a delicate and nuanced way. His is a Christianity that seeks to explain, not exclude, which is a far different enterprise than much of the Christian "theology" coming from the mouths of "experts" on television. Like this:

> The Christian should see two realities at once, one world (as it were) within another: one the world as we all know it, in all its beauty and terror, grandeur and dreariness, delight and anguish; and the other the world in its first and ultimate truth, not simply "nature" but "creation," an endless sea of glory, radiant with the beauty of God in every part, innocent of all violence. To see in this way is to rejoice and mourn at once, to regard the world as a mirror of infinite beauty, but as glimpsed through the veil of death; it is to see creation in chains, but beautiful as in the beginning of days.

Hart reiterates here that the cross was meant to symbolize the overthrow of death, not a sadomasochistic delight in the gory details of that suffering. The cross is not a "validation of pain and death," but the overthrow of both. This is important. A Christian must believe in a fallen world, where sin is an alienation from God, and an unavoidable one according to our human nature (original sin, etc.). A Hart-like Christian believes that people will emerge from the darkness of this age, that God has "willed his good in creatures from eternity and will bring it to pass, despite their rebellion, by so ordering all things toward his goodness that even evil (which he does not cause) becomes an occasion of the operations of grace." Here he makes a distinction between providence and pure determinism. At the root of any desire—even the desire for suicide—is the longing to return to some ultimate, infinite source of all things. Hell, in this vision, is a heart that cannot yield to love. Therefore, it cannot be a product of God.

So, does God permit evil? No, not exactly, although he doesn't not permit it. The restoration of the world cannot rest on the suffering of children, and since we were all children once, it cannot rest on the suffering of people or really any sentient being that is born, lives, and dies. There would be no scales to balance out such an innately unequal equation; there would always be a remainder. I feel for Ivan in *The Brothers Karamazov*, translated into a question by Hart: "Is not this an evil so immense and irreconcilable that it is fixed in the heart of eternity, an everlasting indictment of divine mercy and refutation of divine justice?"

According to Hart, this is where faith, again, is absolutely required. To believe that the world is good, or that there are moments of grace, even if we never see them, even if they never come to fruition. Dostoevsky himself didn't see a lot of grace. After a difficult, lonely life, he was forced to endure an almost execution and then sent off to Siberia in chains. After surviving this exile, he wrote feverishly, but he was haunted and crazed as much as his writing was brilliant and prolific, and he finally experienced a small measure of peace with his second wife before he died. This is the quick biography. I wonder what little moments of his life were graceful sparks of love, ones that either do or don't appear in his books, many of which we may never know, in-depth biography aside. Hart says that "to believe in the infinite goodness of being, one must be able to see it; and this no mere argument can bring about." Did Dostoevsky get there? Can any parent who has lost their child expect to?

We can attach a reason to an event and say it is part of some plan—in Hart's understanding, a reaching of all creation toward grace, the willing of things toward infinite goodness—and also refuse the other trap that claims that all things happen for a reason, so we must accept them. No. Hart's argument is much more nuanced and thoughtful and intellectually interesting than this. Yes, we can say, "It's all part of a plan," but consider:

> There is, of course, some comfort to be derived from the thought that everything that occurs at the level of secondary causality—in nature or history—is governed not only by a transcendent providence but by a

> universal teleology that makes every instance of pain and loss an indispensable moment in a grand scheme whose ultimate synthesis will justify all things. But one should consider the price at which that comfort is purchased: it requires us to believe in and love a God whose good ends will be realized not only in spite of—but entirely by way of—every cruelty, every fortuitous misery, every catastrophe, every betrayal, every sin the world has ever known; it requires us to believe in the eternal spiritual necessity of a child dying an agonizing death from diphtheria, of a young mother ravaged by cancer, of tens of thousands of Asians swallowed in an instant by the sea, of millions murdered in death camps and gulags and forced famines (and so on). It is a strange thing indeed to seek peace in a universe rendered morally intelligible at the cost of a God rendered morally loathsome.

Too right. At the end of his book about that historic and devasting 2004 disaster, Hart talks about watching a man telling reporters the names of his lost children who died in the tsunami when he is suddenly overcome with weeping. Only a "moral cretin" would assure a grieving parent that the loss of a child is part of God's grand design, part of ultimate meaning, or what the universe meant to do, if only this sobbing parent could truly consider what was going on. "Most of us would have the good sense to be ashamed to speak such words; we would recognize that they offer no more credible comfort than the vaporings of the most idiotically complacent theodicy, and we would detest ourselves for giving voice to odious banalities and blasphemous flippancies." Oh, I like him very much. Because that's what people do, and they do it all the time.

We can hate suffering and love God, Hart assures us, but do his arguments translate from the intellectual level to the level of the heart? I'm not so sure. It's possible that my anger at God, my desire for accountability, springs from a quintessentially Christian view of the world that makes specific assumptions about goodness. Maybe. But it doesn't solve the problem of the heart, and how that is made new, if at all. Hearts grow weary, they break, and I don't know—then what?

The world is a horrific place, everyone agrees, and yet we still try to find good in it. This is our task. As Hart says, we must speak, and we can speak to the good without offering excuses for the bad. I've always wondered if that's why Abraham, in the famous biblical story, is asked to sacrifice Isaac: Is it not so much to prove his faith in God as it is to prove his faith in the world? Faith that something—wind, being startled by a hungry goat, a spasm in his hand—might have stayed the knife? A world that would never be the same to him after he'd acted in such a way? Hart might agree, because belief in God and belief in the world are not, he argues, necessarily the same thing. This was a relief to me before my son died, and it is a relief to me now, more than a decade after his death, during which so many horrible events have befallen the world.

Writing about trauma and sadness—looking straight at

it, refusing to look away, trying to make beauty out of the ache of grief—all this is an expression of belief in a world that doesn't reward goodness, but is saturated with it. To believe in something—a story, a person, a community, a benevolent force in the universe, your own mind and heart—all this is creativity, and all of it betters the world, in ways that are both seen and unseen. There's a line in the liturgy of the church where the pastor implores God "to keep and guard our hearts." Although it may sound counterintuitive, I believe that writing about our most difficult experiences is a way of sheltering our hearts. We are protected because we are sharing stories that are hard to tell, but that are eased by the telling, and the telling connects us to those who are listening and reading.

That cold winter in Santa Fe before Ronan died, I ate a lot of sweet Chantilly cake from Whole Foods, feeding him pinky fingers full of frosting. Sunday memories from childhood autumns, the afternoons a blur of sleepy light, Top 40 countdowns on the radio, the whistle of freight trains, dogs barking into the cold, still air. When the sun started to set, we often went for walks toward the mountains dotted in yellow and white from the changing leaves and the new snow. I made weed bouquets for Ronan's stroller. And I thought about all those mothers and fathers of kids all over the world—so many of them, so much suffering—who know or have known or will know how I felt. We are all walking together under the same invisible net. We're all moving down unlit, winding stairs into some new unknown. But that shadow world bumping up against the other one may—or may not—have specks of light. It's possible for grief and gratitude to sit next to each other and share a meal, even if they're never lovers. Cosmic or not, time is passing, things are changing, and people and babies are dying and my son died and so will I and so will you. No reasons, no answers, no apologetics. This is what art does: It keeps and cultivates faith. It keeps us moving down those stairwells into the unknown, finding hope and light and fascination in the people and things and moments you find there. That, to me, is the faith of a creator.

– 6 –

The Joy Index

REMAKING THE WORLD, AGAIN AND AGAIN

What we call the beginning is often the end
And to make an end is to make a beginning.
The end is where we start from.

—T. S. Eliot, from "A Little Gidding"
from *The Four Quartets*

Franca owned a pawnshop in a small town in Nebraska where Railroad Street intersects the loneliest stretch of windy I-80. She had an accent I couldn't place and never asked or learned about, hair dyed a purplish red, a love for lace-trimmed floral dresses with puffy sleeves, and for a time she was my only friend after I wandered into her shop one day in 1990 looking like the sad teenager I was. Most people I knew referred to Franca as "odd" (code for "bad and wrong") because she wasn't married (imagine!), didn't seem to give a shit that she wasn't (what?!), and owned her own store (the nerve!), which was a fantastic, ridiculous mess. I loved hanging out with her in her chaotic, overstuffed store.

Franca's shop was full of abandoned diamond rings (I

thought of her when I pawned my first engagement ring at a shop in an Austin strip mall and used the money to get my first tattoo); piles of Black Hills gold, which was popular at the time; chains of various metals in various states of rust; taxidermic birds and squirrels and other small creatures arranged on top of glass cases full of turquoise jewelry; Union Pacific Railroad work wear from across the decades; and *so many* cross necklaces, thanks to that poster of Madonna from her first album in the 1980s, and the fact that most people in this small Nebraska town were some brand of Christian.

I learned from Franca—perhaps more than any other person—that objects have power, and nothing needs to be discarded entirely; we touch, re-create, touch again, re-create, replenish, replicate. And this has a practical application as well: It's never too late to start again, with an essay, a book, your mind, a person, your life, *you*. Not to make yourself better—that's not the business of living—but to live more happily, more creatively, and with more freedom and joy.

Franca was adamant that this was a pawnshop, not a thrift store, and she liked to talk while she was putting on lipstick, always a dark plum shade, which she did every few minutes. "People bring in what they don't like to get money to buy something they like better. Maybe they trade. Maybe they don't. Maybe they come back the next day." Perhaps she was proud of this circular exchange, which was not just about selling things, but attaching old objects to new owners, continuing the story, tethering an object to the world by changing its owner and its story, over and over again. Or maybe it just set her mind at ease, that she would never be without inventory.

Franca also taught me the power of remaking things: silver spoons bent into funky bracelets, rusted chains polished and fashioned into belts with old locks dangling from the ends, a single suspender from the 1920s transformed into a glittery headband. She used other people's unwanted objects and gave them new meaning, and she gave some of them to me. I had a piece of steel hammered into a textured cross on a heavy chain; a spoon with an engraved *E* that I wrapped around my upper arm like some kind of snake; and a beaded rock necklace that my older brother gave to me for my birthday from Franca's rock collection, which was literally a pile of rocks, some plastic packets of stale-looking rock candy, and then a few necklaces she'd made herself.

Stories—told through objects—can reframe how we see the world and shift our attention in ways that help us find clarity while also making us less miserable. It's a win-win. I walked around weighted down by the creations Franca made for me as if she'd fashioned for me a shield against sadness, which she kind of did. She helped me put myself together, as the saying goes, and it was through her that I found my love of creative expression through fashion, which, in a world where I was the only girl with a body like mine, was a form of preemptive protection. If my outfit was bizarre enough, fewer people would ask me about my leg. This strategy was so effective that it was almost too easy.

What Franca did best in her store was curate a world

where everything had a place and all of it mattered. She made displays of spectacular things that immediately caught our eyes, as if we were inside her mind the minute she saw that brooch or that bangle. I now understand that Franca was one of my first and best writing teachers. One of the writer's jobs is, of course, to make a world of words, images, scenes, photographs—a unique artistic world that acts as the container for the story or the meaning. Each one of us is Franca curating a pawnshop of the mind.

Remaking the world is also a big part of the writer's job. How we see things changes how we understand and enter the story, and objects are a great place to start as an illustration. If you show me a pen, I won't care too much about it. I might snatch it and start making a to-do list. I might steal it if it's a Sharpie. But if you tell me that the pen is the one you used to sign your divorce papers, or your mother's death certificate, it's the saddest pen in the world. Now that object is tethered to a story, and now you can follow that story as it unfolds in your mind and memory. If you tell me this pen belonged to your father and he never wrote a letter without it and you miss him, it's a sad and happy pen showing that grief is the price you pay for loving your dad. If you tell me the pen was a fancy gift from a partner and needs special ink and shows how much this person really understands and appreciates you, it's such a happy pen it might even make Kafka smile. You might have a fancy Birkin bag or shoes that cost someone's monthly salary, but would you trade it for the cheap blue-and-pink newborn hat that went on your kid's head minutes after they were born, the same kind of hat you could find at probably every hospital in the world that is worth maybe one dollar? Would you rather have your crystal glass collection or the weird Polaroid of your favorite person, with a wine stain covering part of their face? Think about it. Examine your objects carefully. If you can remake an object's narrative trajectory, it's easy to move on to more complicated tasks.

Like crafting! Or, in this case, cutting things up with scissors and tossing them around. This is the easiest and most enjoyable craft you'll ever do. In fact, it's not really a craft at all, because I find crafts annoying and mystifying. This is an exercise in making a mess and having fun, and then cleaning it up and making meaning, and then doing that all again *three* times.

I mean this literally: Print the essay or story or chapter. Cut it up into its individual paragraphs and then put these pieces of paper in a pile. Put your hands in the pile and start shuffling as if you were a hotshot dealer in Vegas, and now toss the pieces up like you were making pizza dough and see how they land. Have fun with the paper and with the mixed metaphors. Start moving these pieces around to see if it's possible to arrange the story in a different way as they've fallen on the surface, by chance or fate or whatever. They fell that way; see if there's a new beginning in there you might try as your opening gesture. And now you're having fun, and there's no way you're white-knuckling your computer keyboard or clenching your butthole when you are throwing paper in the air. Tension will make you tense, not creative, but exploring what you don't yet know but might soon is fun and will make you curious. You are now a detective assigned to your own story and you have caught the case. You are a private investigator of your own life and it's Friday night and you're laughing out loud. Do this twice more. In between rounds, you can take a screenshot of your new arrangement or tape it together and put it in an envelope and print the material again for the next two rounds. You will feel silly. You might feel annoyed, you might laugh, you might weep. That is the point. And you will discover something new about your story, I assure you. You might also have some fun.

And it's supposed to be fun. Creating things is supposed to be playful, driven by curiosity (*How about this for the opening line? What if I make this line? What I thought was the end is a better beginning*) and practiced over and over, knowing that stories are living things, and even if they are "finished" and published, they will evolve because new people will be reading them. It's a constant game of *what-if* without the worry and stress we usually associate with those words. So much about writing is about chance or luck: what you happen to see or experience or hear, your mood, your level of physical comfort or discomfort, the time of day, the time you have in a day. Work with that element of chance because learning to enjoy embracing—working with it—is *fun* and fun isn't logical, and logic isn't always your ally in that initial stage of creation. Overthinking doesn't get you where you need to be, and most thinking is overthinking. Playfulness, however, is much more fluid and open, always accessible, and it's going to help you find that metaphor or write that dialogue because when you're having fun, you can't help but relax and stop overthinking. If there's one thing this exercise helps you do, it's to understand how much fun you are to be around when you're not so serious about whatever it is you're doing. This is one step toward becoming a more intuitive writer, which is hard to teach but easy to practice if you're willing. All memory is stored by neurons in a circuit that records; we are, quite literally, wired to remember, which means we're already telling another story, which means we're also wired to rewrite.

When we're playful, we are free to investigate the intersection between imagination and intuition without self-consciousness. Kids do this instinctively; during the pandemic, my daughter, Charlie, then five years old, got off her Zoom school screen and started looking wildly around the room, picking stuff up and setting it down. I heard water running in the bathtub. When I asked her what she was doing, she said, "I'm looking for something that might work as a floating device." *Find a flotation device* was, in fact, the assignment, and she didn't think it was weird at all to search the entire house, because who knows? Her search reflected her belief in the power of curiosity. She also learned the hard way that cats don't float, or at least ours didn't, and that they are terrified of water.

Trust me: I hate crafting and craft parties and anything you fold or cut or paint or poke with a special tool or paste on top of something else. But I love this exercise. In it, I find what I like to call the Joy Index, or an access to happiness while in the middle stages or "middle feelings" of a project, which often feel like a slog. This index or fine line of feeling is different from the high of an idea or the completion of something, and different from the low mood of feeling utterly stuck. It's the frequency of emotional regulation within the artistic process. Instead of dwelling in doubt, cut up paper and throw it around. Story is a kind of systems chaos anyway, so we might as well work with it instead of against it.

There is power and potential and so much joy to be found in a mess. The walls of Franca's store were lined with unlabeled bins and drawers full of bits and bobs that looked like the world's most disorganized hardware store. But if you said, *I need a turquoise necklace pendant that's exactly two inches long*, or *Do you have a neon-green paper clip that will hold twenty pieces of construction paper?* she'd rifle in one of those drawers and find it in five seconds. A woeful mess to most onlookers, which was part of its beauty and charm. Franca knew exactly where everything was; that's how well she knew her world, and she didn't believe that it needed to be perfectly organized to make sense or for the perfect treasure for the right person at the right time to be found. The whole store was like a giant magic hat.

This system of thinking as applied to your writing is also portable. While I don't recommend doing this exercise with scissors and paper on a plane, you can also use the Sticky Note Layer Cake strategy when you're on the road or just in the mood for a different kind of chaos crafting that involves no actual crafting skill whatsoever. When I'm working on a book, whenever I have an idea, I scribble it on a sticky note and trap it on my board with a magnet. I add the notes at random, one on top of the other, and at some point, I peel them off, one by one, and start looking at what I have.

This system is relatively new for me, but its origin story is an accident. I was visiting my friend Emily in London when her kids were babies, and I went to the nanny's upstairs room to ask her a question about how to change a cloth diaper, which was new to me at the time. I knocked, opened the door, and didn't find Renata, but saw stuck to the wardrobe lines of sticky notes—British phrases translated into Czech and vice versa—the edges of which were moving in the wind through the open window. That image stayed with me, the tactile nature and utility of it, the focus and dedication it represented, and the Sticky Note Layer Cake system was born.

A few years ago, on a flight from Los Angeles to New York City, I pulled out my layer cake of notes and started unpeeling them and placing them on my seat back. My friend Margaret was sitting next to me and thought I'd lost my mind. "What is that?" she asked, looking worried. "It's an outline for a book," I said. She was so flabbergasted that she took pictures of it, shaking her head. I organized what I had, typed it all up in a big-ass document, and then threw all the sticky notes away with my snack box. "Wait, aren't you tossing out something important?" Margaret asked. "I don't need the sticky notes anymore," I told her, and she, the maker of the most complicated spreadsheets that give me hives and make perfect sense to her and that she displays on multiple computer monitors *at the same time*, laughed and so did I. It's fun to have friends whose brains work differently.

Later I cut up this same document and tossed it up in the air three times and found the opening (for now) of a new project. I might finish that project, I might not. It might get published or it might not. When you're joyfully engaged in the process, it doesn't matter that much (unless you're on a deadline, and it works for projects under time pressures too). You're doing it for the sake of doing it because it brings you joy and taps into the beginner's mind, the unselfconscious but awake and open mind, where everything is possible, and nothing is forbidden. It's a literary Eden. Who says no to that?

Jack Kornfield describes the beginner's mind as this alert, curious, and nonjudgmental state that invites us "to be fully alive, just where you are." It allows worry and neurosis and judgment to fall away, at least temporarily. And this attitude can be deliberately cultivated by doing playful things, which in turn builds a new territory or mindset: a curious mind that remains interested without judgment or fear "opens a doorway to creative solutions." And when we relax, sometimes creativity is easier than we think. Once on a beach in Maui, I was trying to clear a space for my tent, which is the only place I like to be on a beach, and I kept struggling with deep roots that I couldn't pull out, even when I used my entire body weight and strongest grip to try to uproot them from the sand. I continued dragging my tent around in the sun, finding intractable tree roots. At one point, expecting the twig in the ground to be an Excalibur sword-out-of-the-stone battle, I gave it a huge tug and fell on my ass. Turns out what I had expected to be another intractable root was just a stick sitting shallowly in the sand. I could have unearthed it with my pinky finger.

The up-in-the-air exercise helps loosen the grip or attachment we often have about how a piece *should* be or how we thought it would turn out or how we thought we were going to feel or were supposed to feel while making it. We think, *Well, that must be the opening line because it's been that for three months.* Or *Yes, I need* all *these characters because that's how I imagined this novel and I can't kill any of them off.* A willingness to disrupt that attachment reflex or loosen that grip is incredibly useful in freeing up a piece of work to be its best or finished version. This process harnesses what is already made (what may feel solid) with the power of chance and the way the pieces happen to fall. In that respect, art mimics life in a way that is both liberating and frightening.

Another artist I met at Yaddo visually illustrates the ways in which the unknown and the ephemeral serve your curiosity and therefore your art. This is more than absence through presence: it's the way art and story quite literally stick to us and then are washed away or taken to another place where they become something new. Jinal Sangoi is an artist who, in her painting, drawing, and performance art, works with the ephemerality of art and life through the use of particular textures and materials.

Jinal filmed women in South India for hours as they carefully crafted the elaborate dirt mandalas at the thresholds of their homes. Hours of meticulous placement of dirt within an intricate, symmetrical pattern that they know as well as the back of their hands, each one, each day, wholly original. Every morning, long hours of artistic labor, and then, throughout the day, visitors walk through the mandalas, lifting the patterns into their clothes and erasing them from the ground to be carried in a different form into the house. At the end of the day, the mandala has entirely disappeared. Everything beautiful is ephemeral and belongs to the world from which it originated. At Yaddo, Jinal spent six weeks painting the most fabulous table I've ever seen, full of shapes and color and patterns and designs that was like a child's dream of a worktable. She didn't gesso it, though, and wouldn't because that was part of the point. One tipped-over water glass or awkward splash of wine and the patterns would evaporate in seconds. The art would be "ruined," but that's the point, to challenge this notion in the first place.

All of what we know and love and understand and create is impermanent: this is, according to Buddhist thinking, the only permanence we can trust and it's this unstoppable march toward ruin that makes life—and the art we make of it—precious. What disappears is never lost; it's simply reappropriated, reused, transported somewhere else, transmuted into a new thing that goes on to have its own life, some parts known and others unknown.

And sometimes, as the up-in-the-air tactic suggests, you need to mess your story up in order to give it the space to be what it wants and needs to be, and you must be willing to have each subsequent iteration changed and challenged. I could toss my sticky notes out and cut up a draft because outlines are written in water; storytelling is sacred work that is also ephemeral and dissolves as every other experience does, moment to moment. Nothing is sacred in your art; everything about you that allowed you to create it, where once there was nothing, absolutely is. Every day I get messages telling me ways I can boost my productivity; I'm not interested in that, but I am interested in boosting the Joy Index whenever and wherever possible. Language and poetry offer us an intangible possibility that increases joy if we follow it. We can find joy and delight in that dip into the magic dark of creativity, because however brief the reach, you never know what story might reach back.

– 7 –

Life in the Bone Church

THE ONLY WAY OUT IS THROUGH

It seems to me that one ought to rejoice in the fact of death—ought to decide, indeed, to earn one's death by confronting with passion the conundrum of life. One is responsible to life: It is the small beacon in that terrifying darkness from which we come and to which we shall return.

—James Baldwin, from *The Fire Next Time*

Rome in July is frog-boiling hot. Tree branches, stiffened by the heat, splinter the sunlight and send it scattering across the sculpted and upraised arms of Bernini's Triton, dripping water from his muscled arms and thighs in the Piazza Barberini.

I've come to the train station to meet my friend Julie, and I see her crossing to me from the platforms with her signature face-splitting smile and dark hair: my witchy Irish sister who gives the best hugs and even better advice, comfort, care—all the things you get from a bestie that feels like a sister. I've invited her to Italy during this sweet spot between the waves of COVID-19. I let her have a strong coffee before asking her if she wants to go to the Capuchin Crypt, or "the death church," with me, like right this minute. I saw how close it was to the Airbnb, and I literally cannot wait to go.

"Why not? I love a good wake," she says, and we drop off her luggage and together cross the street to the bone basement.

The Capuchins, who wore tunics with hoods to cover their heads, thus their names, broke from the Franciscans in 1525 to live, they believed, more authentically aligned with the teachings of Saint Francis, who advocated poverty, chastity, faith, and humility as the primary virtues of a Christian life (he also loved animals and advocated for their humane treatment). Pope Urban VIII built the chapel between 1626 and 1631 for his brother, Cardinal Antonio Barberini, who was himself a Capuchin brother. The pope excavated thousands of brothers from their previous burial places and arranged them in the crypt: anonymous recombinations in meticulously arranged, bony grooves of nameless oblivion. In death, everyone becomes a commoner.

Inside the church of Santa Maria della Concezione dei Cappuccini, a series of low-ceilinged, interconnected basement chapels, the air is close and quict, as if someone is breathing carefully in a space where others have breathed their last—in this case, so many others it's impossible to count. Visitors cross the low threshold into this boneyard, but it's a funky, fancy one where everyone is intertwined with everyone else, like trees that cross deep branches underground. It's as if a field of aspen trees, known for their deep and complicated root system, has been turned upside down like the child's game of "open the church, and see all the people" we were taught in Sunday school, flipping our interlaced palms over and wiggling our fingers. This space feels liminal, transitional, and intimate, but also weirdly alive because it requires the viewer's full presence to take in the arresting strangeness of it all—this collection of skeleton bodies made of various dead people's bones, perhaps a glimpse of the great unimaginable beyond. We are living, sweaty witnesses to the cool corpses and shadows and silence we will eventually become. Skeletons are lying around, sitting around tables with no food and only silence between them; some are in a position of prayer and notched into a small cutout within the cave wall. The air is cool and damp and smells like wet dirt that hasn't seen the sun, stale wine, and ink, like something thick to walk through.

The round and shallow rooms hold Adam and Eve–like couples, although it's almost impossible to distinguish sex or gender: that rib connected to another's thigh bone; that head mounted on another person's neck; ribs flaring like wings across the ceiling, as if the room might take flight; elbow joints holding up one side of a bone bed where a skeleton in a cloak lounges until the earth is swallowed by a massive star. A staged jumble of bones, an underground rave for the dead as the unseen DJ plays the silent soundtrack of the past that we trace with our breaths, as if with our living presence we might bring them to life. The ultimate performance art production of the human future, which is to say: death.

Low, arched passageways lined with skulls lead us from

room to room. Flared cages of bone are kites flying from the ceiling. Elbow joints prop up the side of a bed where a skeleton stretches out. Pubic bones fold over one another like a display of napkins in the shape of a stingray; a wall of shingled scapulae spread like a deck of cards over an arched entryway; femurs and fibulas stacked like firewood in a barn; a spray of fleshless fingers hanging from the ceilings; one skeleton, head tipped to the side, standing behind another as if tying a necktie; knee joints stacked like fists in a game of rock paper scissors; sockets without eyes manage—somehow—to bulge.

Each room has the quality of a progressively more bizarre and intricate dream, or a dream just before it tips into an adventure or a nightmare or a bit of both, or a place that appears in your dreams in various forms—a house that is sometimes full of Greek pillars, other times with a rickety wooden porch, but the structure always sits at the end of the same dusty path and gives the same dream feeling, no matter its iteration. It is an encounter with a distant place—hallucinogenic but also concrete—one full of dreams and the edges of dreams that haven't quite been smoothed out yet or have been whipped away, never to be grasped. There is an utter stillness that hangs over everything, which somehow suggests movement by creating the conditions for its total absence. The bones promise "as I am here so will you be," and the perky employees in the gift shop will sell you a postcard or a magnet printed with this missive. I wish I could buy one for everyone I know as an ultimate token of love.

It's been a minute since I've been this close to the physical representation of death, this dusty, infinite stillness; and here, with one of my closest friends, I've never felt more alive. I emerge from the bunker feeling inspired and invigorated and fully embodied and ready to hug everyone.

"Nobody gets out alive," I chirp. "That's life!"

"No, they don't," Julie says, laughing. "And I need another espresso and yes, that's life." And my friend Julie knows all about life and struggle and love and community, having lived and worked in rural Guatemala for over twenty-five years, providing access to education and wellness to hundreds of families at Education and Hope, a dream of love that she started and realized, and that is constantly evolving.

Outside, the light staggering through the midday heat somehow resembles fragments of glass and bone, as if we've brought the images from down below up into the light. Leaves cast shadows that suddenly looked like empty eye sockets, the vertebrae of a spine, a hand. Triton still loomed over his fountain, muscular and ridiculous and everlasting in the sunshine. The triumphant passage from book 1 of Ovid's *Metamorphoses*, the passage that Urban sent Bernini to illustrate, was well known to all literate Roman contemporaries and feels, after emerging from the crypt, hilariously, deeply absurd:

Already Triton, at his call, appears
Above the waves; a Tyrian robe he wears;
And in his hand a crooked trumpet bears.
The sovereign bids him peaceful sounds inspire,
And give the waves the signal to retire.

In Rome, as ever, today's heartbreak is old news. This is true for all of us, even if we're not in Rome. Some heartbreak acts as a superficial cut that runs fast and clean—a lot of blood for what was, in the end, an insignificant wound or a shallow connection revealed to be limerence, a shadow of love but not the real deal. Other breaks and ruptures take us inside the barbed wire of an emotion, into its smoking center, its deep chasm, its hollow skull, and that's where we need to rally. As Rilke says, "This is in the end the only kind of courage that is required of us: the courage to face the strangest, most unusual, most inexplicable experiences that can meet us." Our ability to practice this courage is tested in the face of the unfathomable, the unfamiliar, and nothing fits the bill quite like the biggest and scariest of the unknowns: death.

What does a revelation in a belowground church full of bone people arranged like the Lego constructions that my daughter used to make have to do with writing and creating and telling the truth? Everything. Here is where the power of curiosity takes center stage; it must come forward for its solo, ready or not. And it has a question to ask.

When we're writing, loving, creating, or just being in the world, the most helpful question to ask is *What will happen next?* It is not rhetorical, nor is it tinged with a sense of doom; in fact, this question is eloquent and necessary. It drives the artist *in the moment* to create, change, or move toward an idea, a project, a line, a character's interior world. This question is also essential because we know the answer already: we die. But to know that and to accept it are two very different states of mind, heart, and being. Luckily, we have guides.

The Zen Buddhist teacher Frank Ostaseski, who works with those who are actively dying, as well as the rest of us, reminds us that "death is not waiting for us at the end of a long road. Death is always with us, in the marrow of every passing moment. She is the secret teacher hiding in plain sight. She helps us to discover what matters most." This truth has been a beacon for me in my writing life, but it wasn't always so. After my son's diagnosis of Tay-Sachs, I learned that the rare disease that took his life was a direct result of antisemitism, which, as early as the Middle Ages, led to forced ghettoization and intermarriage, which resulted in the mutation of a gene that I carry. A disease steeped in hate, manifested as horror, slowly peeling away a child's life: sight, movement, cognition, and finally, breath. The first skeleton to greet you in the Capuchin Crypt is that of a child, holding a scale and a death sickle: a message, a warning, a reminder.

"*Radical Acceptance* by Tara Brach," I say to Julie. "Remember that book?" She remembers.

"Someone gave it to me when Ronan was diagnosed and I think I did something really dramatic with it, like burn it in the fireplace or something. I didn't radically accept shit."

"You weren't ready to read it," she says. "And now you've lived it. You could read it now, or maybe you don't have to. Plus, you can just listen to Tara now." And we do, in the mornings, over shots of espresso and twisty chocolate donuts, the world outside the windows warming up as Tara's voice moves like a calm breeze through the tiny cell phone speaker.

"And just knowing you didn't have a choice in terms of acceptance—that you had to do it—probably made you a better writer."

"I think it made me a happier one."

"Really? Why?"

"Because I was free. My last fucks had flown away."

"Well, that is dramatic, but it makes sense."

Radical acceptance is one of the most challenging things we can do, but there's nothing like walking through a basement dungeon full of bones and skulls to remind you that this life is going in one direction and your time is limited. This is part of the human lived experience, which is pay dirt for the artist.

Thinking about death, the great unknown, is frightening, and often addressed in literature and everywhere else. In Tolstoy's *The Death of Ivan Illyich*, when Ivan understood that he was dying, "he was in a constant state of despair." This radical acceptance of mortality is no easy task, but it is an essential one. When you accept the fact of death, you have a password for living life that even the most advanced emotional hacker could not crack.

I cannot begin to count how many conversations I've had with writers and artists when the word *despair* was used in reference to art or process. *Why is making art so hard? Why can I see the novel in my head but it's just not moving onto the page? Why am I doing this?* Try imagining these thought bubbles over skeletons in the crypt, as I did, and you might feel a bit more relaxed, weirdly. Yes, it matters, but also in the end, it won't so much. So better make use of the time you have left, however long that is, and have some faith.

Why *is* making art so hard? Why do we get stuck in our heads and white-knuckle our computers and bitch to our friends about the woes of our bankrupt or absentee muses over pitchers of margaritas? The why, I think, is inextricably linked to two things that also go together: faith and despair.

First, despair. Everyone's favorite despairing and depressed philosopher from the nineteenth century, Søren Kierkegaard, in his cheerily titled book *The Sickness unto Death*, offers a detailed dive into the experience of despair, in which he identifies what he believes to be all its various forms (pro tip: this is not a beach book). Kierkegaard posits that despair is not what we think it is, i.e., a fear of mortal death. Real despair in a man (nineteenth-century Danish philosophers used only he/him pronouns) "is to lose the eternal—and of this he does not speak, does not dream. The loss of the earthly as such is not the cause of despair, and yet it is of this he speaks, and he calls it despairing." When one says they are "in despair," he argues, this is incorrect, as true despair would mean regarding oneself as dead, "as a shadow of himself. But dead he is not; there is, if you will, *life* in the characterization." Hmmm. If it's not the skeletons that freak us out, then what is it? Kierkegaard believed it is a lack of action, a lack of self-reflection, a lack of literal activity.

This is good news for writers and artists, and my interpretation of this bit of Kierkegaard's work is this: *Do the thing.* You are not dead yet; perhaps it is not death you fear, not the passing away of your body or the idea of your bony femur being attached to someone else's knee bone in an Italian cave, or even your empty skull being mounted on a doorframe. Rather, it is the end of the opportunity to create or experience anything new and wondrous. You are in despair at the idea of never again being awestruck, full of unfiltered wonder and delight, not of being struck by a bus, by an illness, by another dead-end relationship. Death in this equation is the end of all chances to *do the thing.* Accept radically that your time is limited, but you do have some until you don't. Accept radically that there is still time for you to make or create what has been and will only ever be *in you.* I'm happy to do some post-death bone swapping with strangers to make a cool skeleton after I'm dead, but in this world, I want what is in my own mind and mine alone—not to control the content, but to see what it can do, make, create, contribute. The mind doesn't give a shit about optics. Neither should the artist who, like an investigative journalist of the heart and soul, is after the truth.

Enter: faith. Another philosopher who cranked out long, serious books at the turn of the next century was William James (Henry's brother), who applied psychological concepts and interpretations to religious experience in his famous *The Varieties of Religious Experience*, a series of lectures he delivered at the University of Edinburgh from 1901 to 1902, a time of massive worldwide cultural and social change, only a short decade before preexisting philosophical and theological certainties were shattered by the horrors of the First World War.

In lecture 3, "The Reality of the Unseen," James says,

> I wish during this hour to call your attention to some of the psychological peculiarities of such an attitude as this, of belief in an object which we cannot see. All our attitudes, moral, practical, or emotional, as well as religious, are due to the 'objects' of our consciousness, the things which we believe to exist, whether really or ideally, along with ourselves.

We cannot see love, but we can feel it. We cannot see or touch an idea or a plotline or a scene from our past, but we can imagine it. We cannot see how our mind works in a moment of creative expression or inspiration, but we can feel it working.

Being an artist is to cultivate a deep faith in the unknown. It is, in fact, the most important prerequisite. What despair and faith (cleaned of any doctrines or dogmas or sanctioned belief systems) has to do with creativity and living a creative life is twofold.

First, nothing lasts forever, and writing or painting or doing any kind of art must carry the brave and grandiose alongside this humility and deep consciousness of the ephemeral nature of *stuff we make*. Like money, you can't take it with you: none of the crypt skeletons are positioned with fleshless hands hovering over rusted typewriters or checking their bank balances on some stone ledger with a bony pointer finger. All the anxious beavering away and intense efforting has come to an end. All is wonderfully still and at rest. Faith is believing you can live a creative, meaningful life before you enter that stillness—no matter what the world says or demands—and that you can find that stillness from which to create, if you practice.

Good news! You don't even have to leap into faith; you can explore the shining rooms of your imagination and trust that there are many things there to discover. You can do it when you're angry, sad, miserable, elated, joyful, tired, hungover, or in any other state. Creating from and within that space can be and is supposed to be *fun*, like unwrapping a present every day, just for you, created by and for you, that you then get to move out into the world, also as a gift. Let's swap despair for fun and see what happens. Let's accept a story we can't know yet and trust that it is worthy of our devotion, our time and attention. Elizabeth (played by Jennifer Ehle) reminds her cousin when she's fussing over how to pack her clothes in the BBC 1990s adaption of Jane Austen's *Pride and Prejudice* that the gowns are hers and she can fold them any way she likes. In these rooms of your imagination, time, meaning, power, beauty, and love are all available—it's all for you, and you can do whatever you like. Within this freedom there is a sense of calm. The Bone Church radiates this calm; it isn't depressing, it's peaceful. It is the absence of any sound but accidental ones. The sound of rest.

As I often say to my students and to myself, "Unclench your butthole." If you take yourself too seriously, you'll never enjoy writing, and the point is to enjoy it. You may think it's despair you're feeling over your creative life, but it's not, because to really despair is to think of nothing at all, to be dead, and you are alive. Write as if your fucks have flown! Be dramatic and take a risk. Who knows what will happen tomorrow or five minutes from now or in the next decade? Create now with joy and uncertainty because you believe in what you're doing, because it matters to you, because it's a gift to the world, and stop pretending like any kind of artistic achievement will make someone or the world love you, or that it will make you love yourself. It won't. This is not self-help or self-care or weaponized creativity cheerleading; it's a vocation, a call, the thing you find yourself doing in the dark when the world is quiet, or on a crowded bus during the day when the world is chaotic, or at a time in your life when the bottom has dropped out of all that you knew or trusted or thought was unassailable and forever. The thing you turn to when life plummets or rises in extreme ways, when you're at a threshold moment or moving through one. If creativity is your birthright, which it is, why not enjoy it? The skeletons remind us that time is limited. Nobody is forcing you to create, but if you are feeling the urge to write or paint or sing, why not? Urges were only off-limits for monks, and even GOAT monk Saint Augustine couldn't get ahold of his lustful thoughts, famously writing in *Confessions*, "Give me chastity and self-restraint, but not just yet." You're alive; don't play dead. Not yet.

Speaking of faith, in A.D. 400 Saint Augustine wrote about the struggle between desire and religious devotion in a book written three hundred years after Jesus died and Christianity was finally accepted within the Roman Empire. His book, still in print, is still considered one of the best autobiographies of *all time* (or all recorded time, that is). Augustine is talking about his pesky sex fantasies while being a servant of what we'd now classify as a Catholic God, as there were fewer versions of God then, as the Reformation was far in the future. Still, the message is clear: You don't have to be perfect. You just need to be alive and in a state of wanting to do it. So instead of despairing, start regarding the world in a new way, in *your* way, through your particular lens that is made up of your memories and wishes, dreams and heartbreaks. Or, as Thomas says in the Nag Hammadi, a precursor Gnostic source text for the Synoptic Gospels that was excluded from the final redacted text for being too radical, "Open your eyes." And mind and heart and ears and spirit. If an early saint, devoted to what was then seen as the highest possible calling, the most pure and meaningful—a lifetime devotion to God—could reconcile himself to not being perfect, so can you.

What would you tell a beloved friend about their projects or creative impulses? If it's not a clear *Go for it*, it might be time for new friends because here's the other thing about the Bone Church: It's not just one giant skeleton. The bones of different people are individuated and then they are arranged in groups, together. Separate but not alone. Writing is and always has been and always will be a collaboration: between the self and the world, the self and others, the project and the world. The Greeks would *not* say the self against the self, because there is no distinction between body and soul in Greek; it is, simply, *soma*: σώμα. The Greeks had multiple words for nearly everything, but the body and the mind share an experience of the world, and that gets one word, all of one piece. *Soma* means "body," "dead body," "one's life in the physical world," "that which is material" (not spiritual), "person" (in general), and "entire thing," or a three-dimensional object in math. Body and mind are inseparable, just like life and death.

As Julie and I walk the streets of Rome and drink fresh water directly from the fountains and get lost every five seconds because the GPS is confused by the winding streets and old buildings ("Where are you taking us, blue dot?" we wonder aloud as it spins and spins inside the ancient alleyways), I'm thinking about death and art-making and friendship—in particular, my first friend, who was an old man. Before I lifted my son, Ronan, into the undertaker's arms on Valentine's Day 2013, my friend's was the only other dead body I'd touched.

Beginning when I was six years old, I often accompanied my father, a Lutheran pastor, to funerals where he solemnly officiated beside a closed casket, sending out prayers of consolation over the bent heads of sad strangers I quickly forgot about. My indifference came to an end when Otto died.

I had friends through proximity of age and geography, but Otto, a friend of my father's, was the first friend I consciously chose. He was a botanist and a creator. Each winter we made Advent wreaths in the gymnasium our church rented for this singular purpose. Otto's horticulturalist's hands—age-spotted and knotted as bark—expertly twisted and bent the evergreen boughs around the stiff hoop of wire. I was a terrible wreath maker; Otto patiently showed me how to wrap the wire, again and again.

While we worked, he said, "Tell me a story." Bible stories were the most familiar to me, as I heard them every week, so my narratives tended toward the epic: witches who disappeared in storms; people forever lost in the rain; villains whose crimes went unpunished; a lot of girls fell into holes and somehow climbed out again with the help of a small and fiercely loyal animal; occasionally someone would say, "I smite you!" Otto offered feedback with nods, appreciative grunts, or comments: "The thundercrack is a nice touch" or "Unexpected ending!" or "Ooh, quite the villain!" I often lay awake at night, spinning the next story for him.

Neither of my parents had known their fathers: in this Midwestern gothic tale, my maternal grandfather, gripped by depression, shot himself in a barn on a March morning in 1944 when my mother was just eighteen months old, leaving his wife and two young children alone and with no money. My paternal grandfather went to war after my grandmother got pregnant as a teenager, and never met his son, my father. Although he was not bound to me by blood or genetics, I loved Otto as I would a grandfather. I would be fortunate to have other grandfatherly figures in my life, but he was the first.

When you have a friend, you notice everything about

them, as if to remind yourself of your great luck. Otto, from Germany, came to the United States as a prisoner of war. My child's imagination pictured him alone and brave and hopeful on a ship in a wild sea. His accent had a scratchy, sandpaper sound. I teased him that he was an owl, with his hoot of a name, and his round, bald head covered in dark spots. He "stood against the Nazis," my father said, but didn't elaborate.

The knowledge of what fascism is and does was still years away. Otto spent hours talking with my father in his church office. I heard their voices behind the closed door while I impatiently waited and tried to solve the wooden puzzle my father left in the vestibule for waiting parishioners. My father saw in Otto qualities of gentleness and kindness that had been absent from his childhood, and that I knew he wanted to emulate, which he did.

I insisted that I be allowed to attend Otto's funeral, despite the warnings that it might be upsetting. I hadn't grasped that death was a permanent condition. Otto's casket was lined in white satin. With its bridal associations, this color seemed a strange choice for a man, especially a horticulturalist who worked with dirt. "White like heaven," my father said.

"Can I touch him?" I asked my father, who nodded yes and lifted me up. I touched Otto's cheek with my palm. It was spongy, chilly, and strange. He was so motionless that I was afraid he might make a sudden movement, for how could anyone be so still, even in death? A tree had more movement. A still leaf. An apple resting in a bowl. This was a different kind of stillness. Final. Absolute. And yet in my mind, not even beyond reach but as if I could watch the scene unfold, I saw his hands carefully wrapping greenery around a wire hoop.

After Otto's funeral, everything felt too singular and vivid. The world had sharp edges and places I'd never noticed before, as if our small town in rural Wyoming held secrets I only saw clearly after something I thought would always be a part of it was taken. A red steeple punctured the shadow of the town's only historic building. Snow weighted the roofs of empty houses. Frozen brown slush blocked the gutters of the streets; the university, empty of students during the Christmas holidays, loomed white and mammoth in the distance. The bars lining the main avenue looked weirdly festive, blinking lights advertising Budweiser and Michelob. Men in tight jeans moved in and out of the doors, belts cinched, boots polished. Years later, a young college student named Matthew Shepard would enter one of those bars and end up beaten and strapped to a fence in the prairie outside of town. Hours later he was found, and he died in the hospital of his wounds. On the day of that first death in memory, the world felt carved out too precisely to be safe; to be a part of it was to be in danger. To love it—or anyone who was a part of it—was to know that they could leave it. Everything could fall away.

My grief for Otto matched my love for him in its depth and intensity, as is always the case. For weeks after Otto's death, I was inconsolable. Most of the funerals I'd attended with my father were for somebody's mother or aunt, their father or sister or brother—only once for a child, where I was not allowed inside the sanctuary but could hear the mother's howls from where I had been sequestered in the basement to read (although I couldn't read a word). The grief I witnessed in those settings made sense; they were *family.* Otto was the oldest man who had ever lived in the world, from my child's perspective, and he was not related to me.

I felt as if someone had thrown a cloak over my usual enthusiasm. I couldn't sleep, and for three nights after Otto's death I read *Little House on the Prairie*, one book in the series after another, curled into the basement window ledge with its view of the skeletons of winter bushes shaking in the high winds. I read all the books save one, *The Long Winter*, which had once been my favorite, full of small acts of ordinary bravery, like Pa tying a strong rope from the barn to the house so nobody got lost in the blizzard and all the animals stayed safe and warm and fed.

But now that book reminded me of Otto—cold weather, kindness, the absence left by someone who is missing. No rope could bring you back from a casket, and death was, it seemed, very much like a blizzard one disappeared into, untethered and wholly lost. I developed a fear of snow. I didn't want to go out in the cold—a challenge during a Wyoming winter. I wore mittens and heavy socks indoors. I swore I'd never have another friend; the pain of loss was too great. I was, at this age, experiencing one truth about grief, which, as Heather McCalden observes, "has no metaphor." I couldn't square my feelings with the reality of the world—everything felt, quite simply, *off.*

I made more friends, of course, in part because Otto taught me the value of being tethered to a person you choose, and who chooses you. Friendship is its own kind of art—of connection and love—and it, too, like all art, is fueled by curiosity, commitment, and care.

All the people Julie and I pass on the streets of Rome seem so helplessly and tragically and stunningly human, and so are we. People chattering on cell phones, going to parties, making plans, having loud arguments, wondering what the day will bring, stopping to window-shop or send a text message, checking items off their to-do list, all the while leaning so obviously into the unknown. It hurts to look at them, so alive and so mortal, but the looking is invigorating too, a reminder of how big the world is, and how little we know about it, and how much it has to offer.

"It's so hard to be a person," I say to Julie. "Sometimes I wake up and wonder if I am actually still a person."

"It so is," Julie says without missing a beat. "And I feel that way all the time too."

"Seeing the bones of dead people helped. Let's get gelato."

"It really did. And yes to gelato."

It was fitting to visit the Bone Church with Julie, who is the kind of person who says to you, "I will love you until the very end, no matter what," and you know this to be true. She is the truest kind of friend, which is to say a person with a relentless and radical belief in your goodness, worth, and beauty, the same belief you have in her.

In one of my favorite short stories of all time, "Taking Care," by Joy Williams, a pastor is caretaking his terminally ill wife, whom he deeply loves. When the doctors can do no more for her, he decides to bring his wife home to die, and in the last paragraph, the man is utterly, painfully alive with despair and love as he carries his wife across the threshold of their home for the last time. Williams writes, "Together they enter the shining rooms."

The Bone Church doesn't have shining rooms—it's a dusty, windowless crypt—but entering it gives me the same sensation as that character in the story, when entered with a friend, or entered solo, in the world of one's mind. Story is the vessel that crosses the chasm of separation that we imagine exists between ourselves and others, between ourselves and the world, between the person we are and the person we are becoming. Death helps us understand the power and preciousness of life, and this is why proximity to death—to those untold stories of the bones in the Bone Church, and the stories the living imagine about them—matter so much.

The Bone Church remains a place of wonder that is strangely absent of terror. The caves offer a deep, if playful and macabre, respect for bodies, and it is in bodies that story originates, blooms, and unfurls. Our bodies are the medium, whatever they look like. All stories are embodied, and all are worthy of time, attention, and remembrance, just like those bones, just like our bodies. All those bodies are now collaborating with other bodies and the memories that are no longer available to us, but live in the world still, in someone's memory, someone's treasured book, an old family story, a museum display under glass. When you write, you are collaborating with others across time and history, but you are also in conversation with all the past versions of yourself, all of which have collapsed into who you are right now, writing and breathing and living, being a friend or a parent or a partner or a child. Life is the most evident and vibrant when held directly against the truth that someday it will be over. In this way, the Bone Church is brimming with vitality and vigor and *life*.

We are all the same. We are all going to die. We are all unique. We are all storytellers. We all seek truth and transformation. We are all afraid. As Frank Ostaseski asks, "I'm feeling afraid, aren't you?" when discussing the cultivation of a deep awareness of the gift and fragility of life. Looking death in the face only emphasizes that feeling of belonging to a world where nothing lasts forever.

There's a famous saying often shared with bereaved parents, or at least one I heard often in the days after my son died: The only way out is through. While this is true for grief, it is also true for the artist. The only way out for an artist is through—the beautiful thing about art, unlike grief, is that we get to make the choice to enter, to go in, to transmute and transform, to be Baldwin's "beacon in that terrifying darkness."

What will happen next? I have no idea and neither do you. Start writing or creating and find out. You don't have forever, but you do have right now.

– 8 –

Rocket Writing

CULTIVATING DISCIPLINE WITH A LIGHT GRASP

> *The true sign of intelligence is not knowledge but imagination.*
>
> —Albert Einstein, from 1929 interview

How do you structure your life so you can *do the thing* you want to do? It's fascinating to think about the creative process, and to consider the possibilities and links to your mortality and embodied experience. It's also helpful to know your why (it is your birthright), but *how* and when and in what way does it get done? How do you stay committed and *when* are you doing this and *where's* your desk? Oh, also how do you manage to get there on a regular basis and tell me all the things I need to do/buy/read/ingest/inhale/experience to be a good writer?

A writer in a beam of light is not a thing, or it might be for five hours or five days or five minutes, but it will eventually disappear. Or, as the writer Bret Anthony Johnston once told my students, "A project will always break your heart at some point," which is why he suggests having two projects going at once so you can flip back and forth between them. Notice he did not say that a book plunged him into a "dark night of the soul," or something equally dramatic. We take our work seriously, but we don't need to take ourselves too seriously, that's for sure. Don't wish for a muse, as inspiration is fickle and infrequent, a relationship characterized by the worst kind of breadcrumbing.

A missing muse is not a problem, because *you* are here all the time, in your body and in your life, even when the muse is not, even when the world is cruel and unfair, even when you are unhappy and don't like the way you look in jeans or can't read the news because it throws you into a helpless despair. Personal discipline is something you can choose every day without locking yourself in a room for five hours or having stink talk with yourself if you don't blaze through a to-do list that is the length and complexity of an ancient scroll. You're in a spiky mood—fine. You're full of rage or sadness—that's okay. You're busy—me too. Everyone is busy with the hustle or the grind or whatever word we choose to describe ambition in late-stage capitalism and/or in a world on fire; everyone gets sad and sometimes despairingly sad and everyone gets pissed off. Everyone understands the world is on fire and feels helpless. Most people who want to write or create do not have large swaths of time and are not always emotionally regulated. Surprise: you're not only mortal, you're also not perfect.

I bet you can discover and protect ten minutes of time. I discovered a way to bring creativity into my day during the most challenging and ruthless years of my life. It wasn't hard to do, which made me initially distrust it, but again, it doesn't have to be grueling to be a good idea. It doesn't have to create misery to generate results.

Rocket Writing, as I call it, takes ten minutes. Let me be clear, this is not about trying to do more with your day, like performing squats while on the phone, or listening to a "how to be a genius" podcast while mopping the floor, or making numbered priorities on your to do list to "optimize" your time and attention so you can do more and work more and effort more. No. You are not trying to mechanize yourself; you're trying to alchemize your emotions and memories and ideas into narrative and story. This is not about multitasking; this is about *single* tasking. This is about ten focused minutes of generating words or images that make you proud and might belong somewhere someday; it's about bypassing the habit of overthinking because there's no time to do so. It's about being realistic about how much most people can actually bear to sit in front of a blank screen and claw story out of the air, which is a bit how writing feels. You don't need to make a spreadsheet unless that's your jam. But feeling something new come from you, crafted and created by you—this is essential.

Before I understood the value of ten intentional minutes, I asked every writer I knew for their suggestions and then I tried to implement all of them, one by one. I was sure the right combination of rituals or the exact replication of the perfect one would help me be more disciplined, get more done, make progress, *be a writer*, which I mistakenly thought would mean that I'd have a place, that I'd belong, for real and forever, in the world and maybe even be rich and famous (whoops—oh well!). Someone suggested I write for the same four hours every morning, no matter what. Someone told me that a real writer doesn't worry about money or health insurance if they're truly interested in being "legitimate." Someone reassured me that I didn't need to worry about being a writer, because I could make babies, which, apparently, he viewed as very similar to writing books. (Absurd as he was, he wasn't entirely wrong: both involve genesis, both require patience, both involve pleasure and pain, both can get messy as hell, etc.) But these responders were all men, all with wives who did the silent, unpaid, and underappreciated labor of cooking, cleaning, and child-rearing, while also earning additional income. If you are also the breadwinner, as most women I know happen to be, I hope this will help you embrace a creative ritual and practice in a new way.

My attention and angst were tethered to the wrong idea: I was worrying about *being a writer* instead of thinking about how I was writing for the sake of the story or to be a part of a cultural, historical conversation that co-creates the world we live and die in. And then someone told me my child was going to die within three years, and some bankrupt personal narrative broke apart and then the art that had been like an albatross around my neck was now the anchor keeping me in the world. It was an activity rooted in and generated by love and grief, and the only way I wasn't totally swallowed up by sadness and rage.

When my son, Ronan, was living in the world and not

just in my memory, there was also a great deal to do and it was carefully timed and repetitive and sometimes it involved complicated instructions, and it was all just really fucking sad even when it wasn't dramatic or scary. To look at his beautiful face and then grab the oxygen machine shoved grief and love too tightly together in the same moment. It was like attending a funeral every day for two-plus years.

Caring for a terminally ill child who may or may not manifest one of the many possible symptoms to manage involves getting up at various intervals for medicine, check-ins, massage sessions, or movement to prevent stiff joints and bed sores. I realized that I had about ten minutes between each of these tasks and so I started writing in ten-minute blocks, demonically at first because I felt like ten minutes wasn't enough time to get out the hundred things I had to write down.

During those ten minutes, and only for those ten minutes, I gave whatever scene or moment or story or idea I was working on my full and absolute and undivided and pretty pissed off attention. I was electrified as a writer, but I was struggling to manage the content I was creating as a person and a mother, even though the act of writing was my tether to joy in a sad world and I was trying not to die. Choosing to be in that space, not for ten hours but *ten minutes*, made the writing better and the struggle of writing about difficult emotional terrain easier. During those ten minutes, pigs could've literally flown right past me and I wouldn't have been interested, even after all that time spent waiting for when they would fly. I felt accomplished because I could manage those ten minutes and still sit next to my son and feel his presence in his few moments of peace. I wrote with intention and focus, and that feeling of accomplishment was motivating. I did these sessions all the time, whenever and wherever, in my phone notes, an old school journal, the blank pages at the back of a book, "Siri, make a note," files, a series of scribbled-up napkins. That's what worked—and still works—for me. With so much input, so many images and ideas draining our attention, it's hard to focus for four hours straight (truthfully, I never could tolerate this), but ten minutes feels doable because it is. And while I don't buy into that whole concept that you can do anything for *x* number of minutes, you can write for ten minutes. Maybe your focus won't be as streamlined or razorlike or the same every day, and maybe ten minutes will feel like ten million minutes or ten seconds, and that's okay too. Also: it's hard to get bored in ten minutes—you can stay curious, and creativity will follow close behind, maybe even skipping with joy.

In this culture, we are told and encouraged to believe that we must break our backs to make progress toward our life's purpose, our dreams, our potential, etc. To earn abundance, we must scrimp and save and work until we fall over or run ourselves ragged. We must find the best deal, find the best partner, live the best life in the best way in the best place after finding the best deals on all the things we think we need to have our best life. We must work and strive and suffer or we won't do the thing, and we won't deserve it if we do. This is fear-based thinking rooted in the myth of scarcity (I'm out of time; I'm getting old; I'm losing out;

FOMO is ruining my life; I'll *never this*, and *never that*), a flaw in thinking that sticks only by tacit agreement. These judgments are harsh and toss a weird word salad of facts and perceptions that nobody wants to sample. Spending ten delightful, focused, playful, significant minutes doing something you believe aligns with your true purpose on this earth: what a privilege. What a kid's wild and noisy ball pit of fun, the best present that takes ten minutes to unwrap because it's so fantastic, a bottomless ice-cream cone. Why not choose joy? Please do! You don't have to suffer all the time to make transcendent, extraordinary work. Why pollute a privilege with the slime of suffering? Everyone suffers enough; enjoy that you've committed to your art for just ten minutes and go all in as much as you are able on that day, at the moment when you choose to sit down. Happily. Grumpily. The work doesn't care, but you'll start to care if you don't show up.

I'm not going to list all the "bad" things you might do in ten minutes instead of creative practice to show how you might be missing out or fucking up. This is not a self-help book, and sometimes a routine that is rooted in discipline and desire isn't up to the moving goalpost standard of *good*. Enough with the self-loathing about how we spend or organize our time. Watch the cat videos if it brings you joy, send all the memes to your BFFs, doomscroll through people's vacation photos, and put designer dresses in your cart and pretend you're going to buy them and then don't, a.k.a. *carting*. But also, create. And read if you want to write and read whatever you want: vampire porn, opinion pages or the obits, a glossy magazine or *The Economist*. You don't have to read *War and Peace* to be a good writer (it's still my favorite book, though); sometimes you just want to read *Star* and look at pictures of celebrities with cellulite. A story is a story, and words are words. Write them and read them. There's no pressure to be *good*.

For the last twenty-five years of teaching, I've heard "I want to be a good writer" or "Is my work any good?" nearly every day. Folded into these questions is this singular question: Am *I* good? We make, remake, revise, restart. But *Is it good?* is not the question. Here's an alternative question: Is it authentic and singular only to me, and will it possibly help someone by making them laugh, or feel seen or understood or acknowledged? Maybe, maybe not, but the intention is pure, so the result doesn't matter, or at least not right now.

You are innately good. Your body is good. The labor of your life is not about being good at anything or proving that you are worthy; it's about being good to yourself, good to your aspirations, and good to the body that makes the art that is waiting and wanting to emerge into the world. A story wouldn't arrive in you if you weren't worthy of telling it (ontology again). *Good* is an annoying word, holding an invisible judgment within it, and my associations with it are not craft related, but they have something to teach us about its potentially combative nature.

Trying to be good is dangerous and not a useful metric. Here's why: First, it's meaningless, because art is always subjective, and yes, there are awards given out every year for the "best of" whatever, but some of that has to do with access and who you know and other mysterious calculations that aren't about how good something is. A person who writes a beach book is just as much of a writer as the person who wins a National Book Award. All books are part of the great big creative literary swamp that never needs to be drained.

Second, the word *good* is easily weaponized. During the first ten years of my life, I had a major orthopedic surgery during each and every Christmas break—something removed, replaced, fixed, straightened, or fused. I can vividly remember some of the physically painful moments, but I don't remember why I was determined to hide that I was in pain. I only knew that I longed for the feedback of *You're such a good girl* after remaining silent through some horrifying physical procedure. Even if it hurt, I fixed my face and/or bit my tongue or cheek, but I stayed silent and felt proud of myself for *being good* and for doing pain the right way, or so I imagined and was encouraged to believe. Of course I wanted to be good. Life in the hospital and then in casts and braces and wooden legs was weird and made me feel set apart and out of place. So here, in this one area, I could be good, I could be the best, I could win. I wore my silence proudly and pushed all the trauma down so successfully that I had to excavate it years later through several unwise decisions and a gazillion hours of therapy.

Praising someone for staying silent while in pain is ridiculous and gross. Bearing pain makes people feel terrified and terrible, and we should be able to express that without being told we're moral failures for feeling so. I tell my daughter to scream her head off when she gets a shot if she wants to. Be a so-called bad patient. Stoicism isn't admirable in some situations; it's self-injury. Pain is not a muse for anything: it's simply all you can think about until you're out of it and you want out of it as quickly as possible, which is why the word *torture* is *pain*'s close cousin. Knowing and showing how you feel and asking for help is self-advocacy, and you'll need that if you want to live as an artist, in community and in the world. Being a "good" writer is not a badge to strive for. Being an ethical, kind, generous, and dedicated writer—yes, *this* is worth working toward because these are real gifts and practices that you can cultivate and that will serve you, versus a moment of social gratification that is harming rather than helping.

What about writer's block? *What if I have a full ten minutes of not writing anything down and am having a kind of literary ritual-related panic attack?* This is an ontological question: if you think of it or imagine it, then it must exist, with or without empirical proof to back up your possibly imaginary assertions. In fact, all creative projects begin this way: an idea of something springing from nothing. A big bang of *what if?* explored on the page or the canvas, a word or a line or a melody that didn't exist and was dragged into existence by your mind and your hand. I've often felt frustrated that (a) I can't write a book in five minutes, as absurd as that seems, because (b) it's all in my head, visually and emotionally—isn't there a way to just download the story from the brain onto some sort of magical invisible drive?

Even a chatbot can't do that, or at least not yet. I think writer's block is real enough that it's *not* something to fear, avoid, or even actively disbelieve as a way of trying to avoid it by trying not to think about it, which obviously doesn't work. Sometimes, ideas need to sit for a few minutes or for a decade, but most will probably gestate in some amount of time between these two extremes. Sometimes writing flows, sometimes it doesn't. We could see this as a block, or we could see it as a step, or we could see it as an opportunity to fall into a new portal of meaning and narrative after a fair bit of frustration. Who knows? Let curiosity lead the way. Sit in front of your computer and just stare into space; maybe you need to be bored for a second, or attached to "no-thing," as the Buddhists say.

If you're curious, you're acting on your intellectual intuition by default, without forcing it or thinking about it. Intuition will rarely lead you astray, and even if it does, you'll still have a story or a song or a poem, albeit one that's different from the one you expected, and that's okay too. Or you might write something that is the story you need to move through to get to the one that you really want to tell. There's no way to get it wrong. There's no way to get it right. Writing is not a math problem. Think about this: a virus is an invasive organism that gets the cells to do its work, which is why half of the genome is of viral origin. Sometimes what feels like a mistake is in fact evolution. What stops a writer isn't a block; it's the heavy brick of ego. We think we're special, but we're not; we think we're worthless, but we are entirely unique and inimitable; we think we absolutely must be whatever our notion of good might look or be like, but we can just be ourselves.

As someone who enjoys picking up heavy weights and then putting them down again—which is not so unlike writing, 99 percent of which is revision—I've come to understand that there are often three phases in the "block" period: the lift, the leap, and the letting go.

Here's how I approach each of these stages, as I understand them, to make them more enjoyable and thus more fruitful. It's supposed to be fun. It's supposed to feel good. It's supposed to be labor, but it's not supposed to feel like someone is draining your creative energy through a straw. Work versus labor: big difference. *I have to work on this pain-in-the-ass novel that will not lead to fame and fortune and a world where everyone loves me* versus *I get to labor on this book of my own creation so that other people might feel more human and not want to die and feel moved and connected across the barriers of time, culture, and history.* AND: I only need to do it for ten minutes at a time. Awesome.

First, the lift. It feels heavy; the kind of writing you must write around to get inside, like the world's worst-tasting lollipop with an amazing candy center. You might write for a long stretch and get one sentence that shines within a page of descriptions and the occasional to-do list that intrudes when you're not paying full attention. It's not efficient but *it is* effective.

What I've found makes the lift stage of writing bearable,

even fun for those ten minutes, is to start with the Big-Ass Document (BAD for short, and also cute). In the BAD, I paste anything related to the book I'm trying to lift up: weird articles, images, screenshots of sticky notes or Sticky Note Layer Cake arrangements, screenshots of poetry memes, something I saw on the freeway that made me think of a character or a moment, song lyrics, tiny tails and tidbits of memory. I don't try to organize it at all in the initial stages. I just add and add and add. Then it's like going to a thrift store and trying to find the cutest, most stylish and original thing for the best price. I make notes to myself inside this document, as a reminder that all literature is, in fact, a conversation, not only with the writer, but with the already evolving thing, which is never flat or static. I talk to myself, I talk on the page, I talk into my phone, I talk to my friend Gina, my first editor. Nothing is ever finished or in perfect form; it's simply in its final form. I've never done a reading from a published work and not changed things as I'm reading aloud. Ever. I even tried to revise as I was recording audio for my third book and the irritated producer finally said, "Lady, you wrote it like this; this is how you must read it." Translation: Stop being impossible.

Second, the leap. This is the moment when things start to do that magical clicking-into-place thing, at least in the moment, or you find the perfect weirdly shaped key for the weirdest lock. You know you're going to win this round of Connect Four. You move a paragraph up from the bottom to the top, you flip the ending and the beginning, and then BOOM. You feel it. You don't need to ask anyone if it's right, because you've been so active and alive and in conversation with the material and with the intuition that you can feel in your body, that you already know. You found it: the perfect leather suit from the 1970s that fits you perfectly, is *silver*, costs twenty dollars, and looks like David Bowie and Pat Benatar had a magnificent baby. There's no way you're leaving that on the rack. You buy it, you wear it, it's yours. In the leap stage, you start to trust yourself. You approach a difficult section and think, *Okay, I've done this before, I can do it again*. Consistency and repetition. Training. Pick it up. Put it down. Repeat. Look at your Sticky Note Layer Cake and move the notes around, throw them up in the air, read them aloud, add to them. Stay in touch with the BAD: Sometimes I read it all the way through or scroll to the count of three and then mess around in the middle. Sometimes I try to polish a section, move it to the top, and then write in big bold baddie letters: **INTEGRATE**. Anything that falls below that word isn't in the same state as what is above. And just like an alchemist, we need to respect that it's not ready to be transmuted. At least not yet.

Third, the letting go. Books are, by their elastic and evolving nature, alive. Once they're in the world, they go on to have their own journey, and readers immerse themselves, interact, and are changed, annoyed, saved, helped, irritated, or pissed off enough to send you a nasty note, or moved enough to send you a heartfelt letter. You wear your silver leather suit to a party and some people think you look ridiculous and other people think you're hot as hell. A reader's reaction is not a reflection on *you* or even the book itself, but rather on what books are designed to do in the world: create connection, conversation, (sometimes reluctant) community, and a bit of bother and disruption. There's no way to control those connections; you are the architect, but your readers are living in the house, moving in and out, and they may or may not like where you put the windows, or how you arranged the kitchen, and they might or might not tell you. Or they might think you've created the most beautiful home they've ever seen, and they could live on the porch forever, and they might tell you that, or they might not. Books outlive their authors (e.g., Saint Augustine's *Confessions*, Virginia Woolf's *A Room of One's Own*, the bible, countless others), extending the life and meaning of individual experience outward into the future while being deeply rooted in the past. Don't read reviews or online comments. Neither the inflation of an ego boost nor the deflation of an ego hit is worth the disruption of your peace.

Lift, leap, let go. And remember that even asking the question *Does writer's block exist?* is both a privilege and a responsibility, no matter your answer. What inspires your dedication and devotion is precious—not in a breakable sense, but in a fluid, expansive way. Storytellers are truth-tellers, magic-makers: it's what we're wired to do, what we're here to do, and what we must do, and if we approach it in new ways, what we *want* to and *get to* do. Life is going to make you miserable and sad sometimes, so when you have a choice, why not choose happiness? You can be disciplined and joyful. Truly. Joy, like yes and no, is a complete sentence. Have courage, which is a relentless and radical belief in your art, in yourself, and in the world. Know that this is going to shift from day to day. If your mind is an airplane, sometimes the view is the giant Lite-Brite of a major city, and sometimes you're flying over Wyoming, and there are only a few flickering lights scattered across what is otherwise a vast darkness. That's fine; neither state of mind is more or less important than the other.

Ten minutes a day: try it. Make a Big-Ass Document that you open, every day, for a prescribed amount of time. Ten minutes might be all you need, or you might look up and an hour will have passed. And then try this, which is the hardest part: don't feel shitty when you don't do it, or if it doesn't go the way you'd hoped or planned. For example, I just worked on this book for ten minutes in which I talked about letting go and not feeling bad for not getting what you thought you wanted, and guess what? I still feel bad. But tomorrow is a new day full of one or maybe multiple ten-minute blocks, plenty of chances to follow where the heart and mind are curious about going, or must go, and that's what matters.

– 9 –

The Time Rodeo, Five Moments of Rupture, and the Care and Feeding of Your Creative Brain

Time
is divided
into two rivers:
one
flows backward, devouring
lives already lived;
the other
moves forward with you
exposing
your life.
For a single second
they may be joined.

—Pablo Neruda, from "Ode to the Past"

The moment I smelled it—a combination of old wood, layers of dust, a new coat of paint smoothed over the last one—I pictured my son, dead now for a decade, but once, fourteen years ago, he was getting ready to be born while I was at Yaddo, an artist retreat in upstate New York. I walked through those woods; I ate at the table in the ornate main mansion, the meals prepared just for us; I wrote and I read and I took naps and I had dreams about being a mother and how my life would change (boy, I had no idea). I devoured Hilary Mantel's first novel about Thomas Cromwell, *Wolf Hall*, and I had strange and sticky dreams. That was two jobs, two marriages, two lifetimes ago. I had been to Yaddo once, in my twenties, long before having children, when I sequestered myself in a room and tried to write for twelve hours a day, which was wildly ineffective.

When I arrived for my third stay, this time with Mantel's *Bring Up the Bodies*, the second book in the Cromwell series, it felt like encountering the ghost of hope, the dream of love, a stage upon which all the actors had been replaced but the set remained the same. The last time I was here, one of the writers in the building across from mine used to write all night, and I'd see his light switch on across the path as he was starting to work, just as I was getting ready to go to sleep. We'd give each other a little wave. That window was empty now, although that didn't stop me from looking through it as night fell. I sent my friend a text telling him I missed our daily exchange. I felt a distinctive baton toss of attention from past to present that seemed to simultaneously split and stitch together the air I was moving through. Fourteen years later, the grief had morphed into other shapes, other sensations, but it remained as solid as the trees that flank the lakes surrounding Yaddo, and my body and its lived experience was the threshold between these two places, the link between loss and life. This is true of all of us—we are never ever in one place fully, all at once, and nowhere else. Every moment that drops holds us in at least two places at the same time.

Grief collapses time indefinitely; it grows up the way children do, in some sense, when in the latter case you can see the former version of your child still present in the current version of her face, all the past versions collapsed into the current one: the newborn kitten face; the chubby, giggling baby with a one-tooth smile; the still-chubby toddler; the leaning-out preteen. We are all a collection of our former selves. As a parent, you love each of these versions of your child deeply and all at once, just as you can love someone deeply even when they're not in the world, or love someone and not want to know them anymore. I didn't die of grief, but it would be a lie to say I won't always be living in it, managing it the way one might manage the worst and most erratic employee ever.

A fictionalized Thomas Cromwell in *Bring Up the Bodies* loses his wife and children to the plague. He barrels on, physically and emotionally exhausted, sacrificing all his time and energy to maintain his station as a rags-to-riches boy who made good in the royal court of King Henry VIII, that demanding and mercurial master with a lot of power to back up his Big Dick Energy. Cromwell wears so many masks in his quest to survive that he loses himself entirely. He never addresses his grief, and so it appears in his dreams and lands on him every morning like a terrible, mean-spirited bird. You can learn a lot about how people expect you to manage or manifest grief by reading bestselling historical novels and running around in the woods while thinking about writing. I know all about masks. I have learned how to arrange my face when I need to.

While reading Mantel's book, which is full of unexpected hijinks, miscalculated risks, sneaky back-channeling in the chambers, and of course a fair share of betrayals and beheadings, I wondered, *When did tragedy start or stop surprising us?* This strange and terrible world full of unexpected disappointments and deaths and struggles. Is it making us stronger? I'm not sure, but my guess is no and that more ease would provide more access to a greater strength than the one to be found through suffering.

During my third trip to Yaddo, I highlighted this line in Mantel's novel: "Death is your prince, you are not his patron; when you think he is engaged elsewhere, he will batter down your door, walk in and wipe his boots on you." I felt weighted by these shadows and "shades," as C. S. Lewis might say. I found myself tromping through a deep forest of memories.

While a student at Harvard, I had two jobs and a full course load, and I lived in Mission Hill (fancy now, wasn't then), as much as an hour-long bus ride away from Cambridge, depending on the time of day. I hardly had time to study; I was so busy trying to afford living in Boston and learning the Greek necessary for my classes, which felt impossible. I had never in my life received a C, apart from in nightmares in which I am trapped in my high school, forever ungraduated. So on many mornings as I waited for the bus in the bone-cold air in front of Our Lady of Perpetual

Help, scribbling in a notebook, I imagined how much easier it would be to become an artist or a writer or anything at all if someone else was footing the bill. (This snapshot is itself a privileged example of my point because I didn't get to Harvard by myself, although scholarship kids don't come from families with buildings named after them, so there's that too.) Does struggle breed character or just resentment? Again, I'm not sure. Why do we have the expectation that it should? Would it make us all feel equal to one another when we know that class is the great divider? Would we stop telling people who are struggling that they're having character-building experiences, when in fact they might be struggling under systems of oppression designed to make them do just that?

I know that "character-building experiences" produce one thing for certain: ghosts, and some of them are nasty and long-suffering, while others are woeful and elusive and somehow more annoying. In Hilary Mantel's account of Cromwell's role in the fall of Anne Boleyn, our elusive hero is truly haunted. Cromwell, the working-class roughneck who escapes an abusive father and a dismal financial future to travel the world before finally rising to the top of the royal court ladder, but not without whopping loss. Loss of virtue, loss of the sight of the boundary between cruelty and mercy, and finally, in a matter of days—minutes, in fact—his whole family except one son lost to the plague. The dead walk through the book, float at the top of staircases; they visit Cromwell at night in his candlelit study, shrieking and asking questions, every bit as scary as an overhead parade of bats, appearing, as they do, when he least expects or can afford to be bothered. His living son, the lone survivor, asks, "Where do the dead live now?" Nobody knows. But they do live, inside the grief experience and then beyond it. And in the end, it is grief that makes us equal to one another, at least for a moment, precisely because it collapses time.

The Corporation of Yaddo in Saratoga Springs, New York, is an extraordinary place where at different times in my life for weeks and months I was fed and coddled as a writer (and by coddled, I mean not having to do anything but eat, write, and sleep). The very opposite of hell. Yaddo was started by a wealthy family of the old New York guard. Heirs to staggering wealth. Privileged in every respect. They lived in a bespoke mansion overlooking the rose gardens, where writers and artists now stroll with sketchbooks and notepads looking wistful and bemused. Yaddo has hosted Sylvia Plath and John Cheever and many other notables. People still drive upstate from the city and wear fancy hats to watch the ponies. Skidmore College, the local liberal arts institution, comes with a high price tag for an undergraduate education. My friend Kate, who graduated from Skidmore and who was my roommate in Boston, tells a story about the time she visited the campus with her father, who died of cancer before she was a freshman. They drove all around town, into the parts that bore no mark of privilege. As they drove, he told her that he was proud of her for getting into such a good school, but he wanted her to remember that other people lived in this town as well. I love that story.

Yaddo, the opposite of a prison in every way, is a series

of mansions and "lesser" mansions enclosed and set apart, hidden not behind wire and electronic gates but by massive, centuries-old trees that line the highway. People in town who have lived there all their lives don't seem to know it exists, or they have forgotten about it, as if the buildings float in a kind of Brigadoon. Visitors are allowed at specially appointed times and only with permission. Meals are served at the same time every day. There are quiet hours (although no lights out in deference to those who work the writer's night shift). The idea is that if you allow creators to create without the impediments of the "real world" (bills, cooking, jobs, laundry, other people, traffic), they will be reformed and inspired, and they are. The crucible works. These artists stop procrastinating and complaining about how hard it is to create, and actually do it. They do what they're supposed to do: offer gifts to ordinary people, the "other" people Kate's dad beseeched her to remember, as well as the well-dressed people in the box seats and fancy bandstands of the world.

Yaddo itself was born from grief. The community became a playground for creative minds because Katrina Trask, the matriarch of the mansion and its well-maintained grounds, lost *all her children* in infancy or childhood and she needed something to do with her hands, her mind, her heart. She created a place where you can sit in your room and write while listening to someone composing music in the next room. Where you can go for days without speaking to anyone but yourself and the characters that populate your imagination. Where people bring you a heater if your hands are cold, or a fan if your room is too hot. Someone changes your bed linens and cleans your room once a week. A training in silence and concentration, Buddhist-like and private, but also communal in the sense that you never lose sight of all the other people beavering away at their beloved projects in all the houses and outbuildings.

Grief—like social class, perhaps its sociological equivalent—is the greatest divider, but it is also a leveler. Not everyone is going to "raise their rank" or be born with one, but everyone will experience grief. Even Thomas Cromwell, drowning in riches near the end of his life, is visited by it. Katrina Trask knew it for most of her life and built a monument to it and to art. Money and power will not protect you, but the American bootstrap myth is that they will. You may not have to work three jobs to put yourself through school, you may be grandfathered into a great job, you might be a modern-day-Trask-family-level rich, but someone you love will die on you. Count on it.

I remembered walking around those lakes while I was pregnant with Ronan and thinking, *Geez, this is depressing. These stunning lakes named after dead kids! What a bummer!* Even the name of the community came from the mouth of a ghost: one of the Trask kids, long dead, who thought *shadow* was pronounced *yaddo*. The hulking mansions and dusty rooms are full of shadows, as are the surrounding woods. And Yaddo is beautiful, especially in the winter, when ice traps the leaves underneath one another; they move beneath you and the ground feels unsteady. Each lake bears the mark of a missing child—the air is hushed, the shadows thick and deep. The trees are monumental and ancient-looking and the felled ones cast their long shadows on the surface of the lakes. The air is deceptively still. The low sky, the hum of traffic on the road, the sound of your feet on ice, then dirt, then frozen leaves, your heart walloping against your chest. You aren't the first person here, you won't be the last, the dead and the living are always switching places, like those court dancers in Cromwell's time, taking hands and letting go, gliding across the ballroom to the next partner. The place is haunted, if ever a place was, the air charged with loss, but not in a frightening or desperate way. You don't feel like clawing your way out of it; you feel like walking through it. In November 2009, I walked many hours in those woods and around those frozen lakes, cradling my huge belly as if it were a basketball and I was about to make a bounce pass. In the early spring of 2023, I did the same, with a premenopausal belly and a new commitment to running. Grief is always in translation, changing its borders of power and privilege, like someone playing a game of *Risk*, with your life, a new army invading all the time. Grief makes us feel like we are severed from the world, very much alone.

This is also a myth, of course, as tenacious as the American bootstrap myth that we can rise to the top—whatever that means—via hard work. We can change the topography of our inner world with thoughtfulness and intention, and we are never fully separate from our world. The shadows and ghosts will still show up, because they are part of this whole process; they show us how we are never in one narrative time frame, which means we have access to our memories, our dead, our future, and the scene directly in front of us. We are, in fact, never alone. Time is layered, and this needs to be reflected in narrative. How to do this? Go to the rodeo. The time rodeo!

The time rodeo is not a rodeo, per se, although I got the idea about layering narrative time at an actual rodeo in Sheridan, Wyoming. I grew up going to these bizarre community events full of dust and butts in tight Wranglers and Budweiser in plastic cups, and my brief childhood aspirations of being a rodeo queen were squashed by being too weird-looking, but I hadn't been to a rodeo as an adult until the summer I turned thirty and briefly dated a cowboy. It was the fulfillment of a secret high school fantasy: a man with a decorative belt buckle, a cowboy dress shirt with fancy pearl buttons, even fancier embroidered boots, and very tight jeans just on "the verge of being obscene," to quote Prince, a.k.a. excellent. He wore a cologne that smelled like fresh grass and MAN. I loved to watch him shoe a horse and throw a rope around. I also learned some key rodeo terms, and because I was writing my first book at the time, they began to make sense to me vis-à-vis the process of rendering time.

For example, the header is the first cowboy up to bat (or to rope, as it were), with the goal of roping the steer around the horns. The heeler is the second to rope, hoping to rope the steer around the legs, but this depends on how successful the roping went with the horns and the header guy. The writer is the cowboy or cowgirl or cowperson—attentive, in motion, with a clear objective to harness a bull/story, butt planted in the saddle of their life. Meanwhile, the animal beneath them is in constant motion, creating an additional challenge, because the bull is also a moving target. Time is of the essence, literally, and there's a great deal of pressure within that compressed amount of "on the clock" time, but there's no way to accurately predict which direction the bull will lurch next, or how the horse (i.e., the situation of the writer's life) will move and respond. All elements in this scenario are very much alive: the cowboy who needs to stay on the horse, and the bull, who resists being caught until he doesn't. Within the confines of the corral, there are *at least* two things happening at once that you can clearly see. We want and need that same simultaneity in narrative for it to feel textured, tense, juicy, surprising, and in motion. "Sometimes the bull wants to be caught, and you can kind of tell," my cowboy tells me. "And sometimes, well, it's a real struggle." When I asked him if cowboys had considered wearing padded shorts like pro cyclists, he looked at me as if I'd dropped from an alien ship.

Narrative layering is important in avoiding the tyranny of "and *then* and *then*," as it's often described, a narrative track that is relentlessly chronological and therefore lacks depth as a result. If two things are happening at once, you'll need to give the reader grounding and anchoring details so that we can tell the difference between these two different types of time. The Greeks had two words for time, and an investigation into each is useful as applied to the time rodeo. *Chronos* is a way of marking the space of experience (this happened or is happening within this marked, measurable, sequential period of time), and *kairos* is a more general description (what those happenings mean in a broader sense) in a way that is, by its nature, both limiting and expansive. *Chronos* can be divided into specific units of time, and *kairos* is a specific, qualitative time-tracking experience in a nonlinear way. *I got my Pfizer vaccine at 4:00 p.m. on March 31, 2022, during the time of COVID-19* mixes these time states. Language itself, which expands and limits the ways we understand or misunderstand each other, lassos the time together: what just happened happens again in the recap. Past memories are linked with current reflection. This time container that holds both *chronos* and *kairos* is like a big squeeze—a rupture—where both realms of time are present because of unrest or swift or dramatic change; this container holds meaning while also pressing it out through the puncture or rupture the event created.

Layering time is just that: a rodeo of folding together dialogue, action, exposition, and the narrator's interior thoughts, and then offering reflection from a near or far distance that lets the reader know why this is important on a wider scale, and not just as a part of a linear chronology of causation where A leads to B leads to C. Instead, it's *I did this* and *I felt this* during that doing; now, this is what it means to me having gone forward a little bit—or a lot—in time. Chronological on some level, but also associative. The time rodeo: balancing *chronos* time (by-the-clock time or how many minutes one stays on a horse in competition, for example) versus *kairos* time (the time of the barrel races) with the way language is used to render that particular experience (the announcer's postscript).

Any rupture is a challenge or opportunity to our sense of identity as well as our sense of time. We all know our time is finite, but we are wired to build value and meaning around our connections to ourselves and to a singular other or multiple others. When the landscape is ruptured—the end of a relationship, a death, an illness, a job loss—we struggle to find orienting landmarks within this new terrain. Our house is wild and the bull is erratic; we are a moving target trying to capture a moving target and also it's raining or snowing. Time suddenly has a climate, which is annoying, because climates are unstable, changeable, and subject to ruin. But it's also true to the nature and unpredictability of time, even as it is precisely marked out *ticktock* like the beat of your heart.

What is the lasso, then? Language. At the rope and saddle store in downtown Sheridan, you can find a kind of rope for every type of rodeo activity or ranch work. The walls are lined with ropes, like dusty snakes in a state of stillness; they are braided or smooth, skinny or thick, all constructed differently to do a different thing. It's like a visual representation of utility, which is the job of a language lasso: it should be beautiful, clear, descriptive, musical, wrenching—whatever the story needs, whatever serves the story. Some of the lassos are more pliable and softer than others; some feel as unbreakable as steel and are meant to withstand a certain animal poundage or amount of stress; some look like fire hoses but are not as heavy as you might expect.

"What if a rope breaks?" I ask the man at the counter

that day. The whole store smells vaguely like leather, animal, sawdust, and tobacco.

"Most ropes can be repaired," he assures me. "Ropes are awesome."

Indeed. There are saddles at the store too, because those serve very specific uses for a rancher or a cowgirl/boy/person. On the ranch and in the rodeo ring, everything has a purpose. So, too, in narrative.

That summer, lying in the bed of my cowboy's truck in a field, the sky was a bright display of constellations easy to identify: the Big Dipper, the Little Dipper, Orion. These long-dead stars had been holding down *chronos* time for thousands of years and also the *kairos* time of life on earth and here we were, in this singular moment, listening to Merle Haggard croon about the way love goes. Constellations of time and memory, both known and unknown. Two eras of time, collapsed here, collapsed everywhere, all the time, all over the world.

A visual artist who engages directly with the concept of time and spatial orientation, as well as the ephemerality and/also foreverness of art is Cuban-born artist Felix Gonzalez-Torres. My brother James and his husband, Robby, co-sponsored a 2024–2025 exhibit of Gonzalez-Torres's work at the National Portrait Gallery in Washington, D.C. James describes Gonzalez-Torres as "a modern/contemporary twentieth-century artist whose work combined often minimal, conceptual, and interactive art in ways that could speak to both public and private experiences in deeply personal, emotional, and political ways. His art drove conversations about what mattered in the moment, and what would matter in a timeless way."

Gonzalez-Torres insisted that the installations be curated differently each time they were exhibited. Many of the installations have pieces and parts that can be taken with the viewer, beyond the museum, out into the world, into places unknown. The materials themselves are familiar, known, and ordinary: light bulbs, wall clocks, stacks of poster-size papers, wrapped candies. Where the items may end up are unknown. My daughter took a piece of wrapped candy from a pile and kept it in her pocket for two days, and now, still in the wrapping paper, it sits on the shelf of the vanity where she does her hair every morning before middle school. But Gonzalez-Torres wasn't prescriptive about how the art could be moved or where it could go. If Charlie had left it on a bus or eaten it and thrown away the wrapper, that would be perfectly in line with his vision as well. There's no right arrangement for the art, and there's no right way to hold it or take it or keep it or lose it.

The point is that all art is fleeting, and because this is in fact the *only* certainty of time, his art is timeless in a very particular, very generous way. I have a photo of Charlie, in a hooded fleece bear jumper standing under the lights of an installation, her ten-year-old face locked in a direct gaze at the camera, illuminated by lights that cling to the doorways and are left to pool and tangle on the floor. She is captivated, and there is wonder and delight in her expression. The work of Gonzalez-Torres crosses the boundaries of time and experience in that way, showing how art is as much a part of the world—and thus subject to chaos and chance—as it is separate from it when carefully installed in a museum. Both/and versus either/or.

All this crossing and layering of time begs a question: Which moments or beats to choose? Nobody wants a kitchen-sink novel or a three-thousand-page memoir (and no, it cannot be split up into multiple volumes; I don't care what you did or how interesting you are—just no). I use what I call the Five Moments of Rupture exercise, which activates these time periods and allows you to layer time in a way that also roots you in the moment of your life. It's not an easy blend, but it's a lot easier than trying to lasso a bull. This is how you do it:

First, give yourself a question. *If I had to tell my life story in five moments, what would they be?* Or *What are the five events or happenings that this chapter or essay must have to say what it is I'm trying to say?* Or *What are the five things I must know about this character to help them feel fully alive in my mind and therefore on the page?* I think of these five moments as ruptures because they effectively blow up your timeline, a timeline that would otherwise flow in a harmonious, fairly dull fashion.

Second, write down the first five that come to mind, without judgment, and without overthinking. There's *no wrong way to do this.*

Third, look at your list, and one by one, take each moment (even if you're confused by why it popped into your mind) and spend fifteen to forty-five minutes (set a timer) doing a massive sensory and concrete detail dump about it. You don't have to make complete sentences. Just think, *Smell, taste, touch, sound, feeling.* Try to remember the light, a smell of something cooking or burning or a certain cologne, a line from a song, a sudden noise, a snippet of dialogue overheard entirely out of context that might be a clue to why this is a moment of rupture you thought of in the first place. As you deepen the senses, you'll sharpen the lens. Move from one to the next without editing.

Fourth, set it aside for an hour, a day, a week.

Fifth, take it out and read through it. For each moment, try to assign an image or a title (especially if it's a chapter) that might indicate visually or otherwise frame what's going on in that moment in a *kairos*-esque way. Some examples of images from former students: a rocking boat, a series of fireworks, a thick crystal vase. Standout chapter titles include "Grace Period," "My Year of Reckoning," and "The Last Man."

I do this exercise all the time on my own. Once, when writing my third book, I kept getting *banana.* Was I hungry? Was this a weird flashback to the sex ed talk I had with my mom, when she showed me how to put a condom on a banana? Was this about my mom? What the hell? Because *banana* kept tumbling out of my mind, I stayed with it. As it turns out, it was related to the shape I imagined my book to be (a boat), and the feeling I wanted the reader to have (a slow rocking, not a totally smooth journey, but also no big waves to navigate). I wanted the reader to feel held but also remain alert. My mind couldn't find *canoe*, so it stopped short with *banana* as if to say, *This is the best I can do right now. Take it and figure it out.* Your creative brain knows what it's doing; it's part of the writer's job to deeply trust it, even when it makes no sense.

This exercise works because it harnesses where you are in *kairos* time—a moment that was part of a stage or period of your life—and then asks you to drop into *chronos* time and offer deeply specific and very particular details within a temporal, causal framework. At Yaddo, a decade after my son died, and the first time I'd been there since, I felt the distinctions between time acutely because I felt a wave of grief—a compression, a tight space. The place where memory and imagination meet *is* story, *is* life, and so this grief was also spiked with joy because it felt alive, fresh, malleable, and mine.

The soul lives in *kairos* time; I felt my son at Yaddo almost a decade after his death the way I did when he was not yet born, and I was writing in the glassed-in porch of a cottage facing the lit windows of another writing cottage. All the hopes I had for Ronan were present in the slow shake of the trees, the parting of the clouds, a revelation of blue color in the sky after a snowfall; and they were still there, even though he was gone, from my body and from this world. The body lives in *chronos* time because it is mortal. But the *kairos* time of love is eternal, or that's what I believe.

There's one more step in the Five Moments of Rupture exercise. Now that you've got five points to work with, the labor of reflection will be your final lasso. In this step, you will break the time-space continuum established in *chronos* time with the block of reflection, or the "why this matters" section of narrative. Analogously, after a cowboy is done roping—successfully or unsuccessfully—the announcer, who was watching carefully, does a little recap of what went wrong and what went right. Sometimes, the rupture is in the repair. If you consciously create these time rodeo ruptures, the story will stitch them together.

This exercise is all about giving your creative brain a task (rope that bull!) but also flexibility (you're on a moving horse and you're the one with the rope). It's also about giving your creative brain somewhere to go around the corral, which means you can't be an asshole to it.

During the pandemic, my daughter, then seven, announced that she wanted a bearded dragon called Hilda. I didn't do the cool-kid pandemic activities like making sourdough or learning a new language. Instead, I watched *Game of Thrones* for the third time and still had no idea who everyone was and what they were doing and why or how, but every time the fucking dragons showed up on the screen, I lost my shit and started weeping. It didn't matter if they torched a town, ate someone or burned them alive, or were mean to their mom who birthed them in a ring of fire: I was TEAM DRAGON.

When Hilda arrived in a little box with air holes, she was the length of my palm. If I left her there, she'd die, but I was worried about not getting the heat and light right in her enclosure, which might lead to her discomfort or even demise. It was a little bit confusing to set it all up, but I managed.

Your creative brain is like a tiny beardie that arrives in a bag in a box in your lap and asks you to take care of it to the best of your ability. Like a dragon, it is ancient, super tough, fragile, and eats live bugs and small pieces of salad. (A dragon chomping through a piece of lettuce or side-eyeing a worm is as fun as an image from a children's book.) I had to be so gentle, and your creative brain also requires this—for us to be gentler than we think we can be and still make art (note I did not say, "Be productive"). As my friend Julie often says to me, "Be nice to my friend," meaning be nice to myself—me, I'm the friend. Telling someone, "I have nothing but love and respect for you" while not being loving and in fact actively disrespecting them is the emotional abuser's version of a gun lover's response to victims' families after a mass shooting: "Thoughts and prayers." People will do this to you; don't do this to yourself. Your creative brain has firm and unassailable boundaries even if you don't in your life, and it refuses to activate or engage if it senses a whiff of abuse or nastiness. If you treat it like shit, if you berate it, starve it, don't give it room to stretch or breathe, or tell it that it's not doing enough or just plain isn't good enough, it's out; like a creature requiring your attentive care, it withers and dies, maybe hides under a rock until it's safe to emerge. It needs to be fed and watered like a child or a plant, or anything living for which you are responsible. If you shout at it, best of luck. Making yourself suffer will not produce art. As Tara Brach says, when we let our storytelling minds tip into negative bias, we are "led away" from our "essential goodness." There are enough wars in the world, so why be at war with ourselves, especially in the making of art, which is a reflection of the beauty and struggle of the world, a reflection of truth?

Art acts as a mirror for the best and the beast in you, and it's important to love and appreciate both. I ask my students to bring in a hot mess of a project because then we're *work*shopping, a situation where people are working to make a piece better; everyone is invested because the writing is a living thing. We are elves in a workshop, but instead of making toys, we're making narrative. I give grades for *talking*, not for participation, meaning talk to the writer, talk to the piece in front of you, talk about how you saw yourself in it, and how you didn't and why, talk about the world. I ask students to do "feel and steal," for everything they read. How did the piece make you feel? What element or method might you steal for your own work? And if you're the writer submitting, be willing to break whatever you've brought into workshop down to its bones once again. You won't learn how to create by hearing only praise, but you won't do any creating if you tell your creative brain that it's a fucked-up loser and not as fast or as cute as the other brains.

Collaborate with friends, collaborate with books, collaborate with cringe. During the pandemic, my friend Lisa and I would pick a word: *leg*, *body*, *leeches*, *sex*, or other words that made us nervous in some way. She'd write a paragraph and send it to me without editing, I'd write a paragraph in response, and then we'd switch twice more and read it out loud to each other on the phone, suggesting real-time edits. Find a friend to do this with, someone you trust, someone you love, someone who makes you laugh and takes you seriously.

Many people are involved in the building of a book or an essay or a story or a novel (editors, other writers, agents, friends, readers), just as many people are involved in the creation of a life (lovers, friends, partners, children, ex-lovers and ex-partners, parents, people in the PTA, randos you meet on a train and make out with when you're twenty or forty-five, a person you meet once as a child and always remember). Art and life: both a series of long and extensive conversations. A rodeo that never rests.

Your creative brain also needs to be nourished, fed, supported, and told again and again that it's doing a great job. It needs fuel, and it doesn't have dietary restrictions, so feed it whatever it wants. Sure, you might want to reread a Dickens novel or read *Madame Bovary* in French—go for it—but stories are everywhere. Watch the amazing Polish movie *Johnny* about a real-life priest who helps people die with dignity and love, transforming the lives of everyone around him. Also watch movies where Jason Momoa or the Rock save someone—or the world—in peril and/or hang out of a skyscraper window and/or a plane. Everyone is always telling me to fill my car with expensive gas, which I think is dumb and I won't do. The car runs just fine; I'm just a terrible driver and I'm messy—the car will last as long as it lasts. Everyone told me my brain would descend into mush if I wasn't reading the latest great American novel the minute it was released or practicing Spanish verb conjugation and conversation in my free time. My mind is just fine for what I need it to do, and I watch crime and action films with nothing less than *gusto.*

Your creative brain has been waiting for you to blast Cyndi Lauper and Marvin Gaye and Bad Bunny or whatever music is your favorite and just have some fun and not pump intellectual iron every minute of every day. In fact, make a playlist for your project; I do this now for my writing students and they love it. Who wants to go on vacation and make each day just another to-do list to walk through? If you want to read something deeply literary, then do it; if you want to read a trashy novel, do that. Relax the grip on thinking you must do one specific or radiant thing to be a smart person or a good writer or a working artist. One great thing about being an artist is that we get to choose our preferred tasks—we're not paying bills or doing dishes or taxes while we're creating, so don't treat it that way. Work versus labor. We're here for the labor, save the joyless effort for the chores.

The Irish writer Aifric Campbell gave me this advice at Yaddo fourteen years ago: "You need some elastic time around what you do. You can't just push and push and push." I liked this idea and came to imagine my workspace and work time as more open and flexible, like the space inside a rubber band that might be pushed out in many directions. "You have to let yourself enjoy exquisite attention. You can't do that if you're always busy."

When a writer can't stop looking, that's a clue to keep looking (unless you're staring at someone with a body you don't understand, and then it's rude). When we were little, I used to put Cheerios in a zigzag line all over the house and watch my dog, Muffin, follow it with relentless focus, gobbling up each little whole-grain circle like it was the first one she'd ever seen and the last one she'd ever eat. Follow the Cheerios. When something stops us, arrests our attention, snags and pins us to the moment or the sound or the scene, we follow it. This is a sign that the creative brain is relaxed and receptive, and it will guide you if you treat it nicely and trust that whatever pulled your total focus is worth being curious about and investigating. This is a moment of exquisite attention, the moment when the lasso lands perfectly. Blink and you'll literally miss it.

This means going out in the world and doing nothing on a regular basis and with no agenda. Wander around a museum (I suggest the crochet museum in Joshua Tree and the wooden boat museum in Seattle, among many others), without taking notes or trying to have deep thoughts. Sit in a coffee shop and people-watch without taking notes or creepily recording their conversations (which was an exercise I was given once in a writing class). Don't take notes, just *pay exquisite attention.* See what snags your attention, turns your head, arrests your eyes or your ears, keeps you to the moment. There is more about the world that is interesting when you treat it this way. Then just let the image or the moment or the information sit there, without trying to force meaning onto it. Just see what emerges when it's soaked in that interesting homemade soup of thoughts and the subconscious machinery of your brain, which is like a Swiss clock, only it tells its own time: yours. It is in this process of relaxing and dedicating ourselves to absorbing the world around us that we will find our own best creative practices and anchoring rituals, and by extension our projects will be less outcome-oriented and more process-centered. The lesson is always to surrender and allow. The road to happiness and joyful, curious creation is always paved with rest and kindness to oneself.

"The things you think are the disasters in your life are not the disasters really. Almost anything can be turned around: out of every ditch, a path, if only you can see it." Thomas Cromwell–cum–Buddhist in a novelist's brilliant imagination. A path through the woods, a traversable route through the darkness. But don't think that the path is easy to find, or easy to walk, or that it won't change you in incalculable and often brutal ways. Notice that there is no promise of being stronger, just a promise that there will be new life (perhaps) after this part of life is over, just as the lake named after a dead child has been remembered by all the people who walked around it. And new life doesn't automatically imply happy life. It will be, as the Buddhists say, what it is. Sometimes you rope the steer; other times you don't.

Are you grieving? Are you struggling? Are you really fucking angry about the systems and situations and so-called leaders trying to destroy people and crush dreams and ruin the world? Is there a story you need to tell from the deepest part of yourself, the part you're worried that others won't want to hear about or from, that you think is ugly or strange? Here's what I learned from Mantel's Cromwell and Katrina Trask of Yaddo and rodeo cowboys. Don't worry about how other people might perceive your process or what they think of you. Don't worry about the quality and texture of your heart. Don't worry about inspiring anyone, or how to be a model of someone else's idea of resilience and survival. Show that you are broken. Let them see you sweat and scream and do a bad throw. Own your disaster; make it into a lake, build for it a shrine—not to show your strength but to show your weakness, which is a way of showing that you are still human, that you are not yet lost. Shine the sign of your struggle into the sky. Lasso it into story. Trail it around the room and out the door. Light it up. Take it with you and let it change you. Let it move in the world and change it.

— 10 —

Patterns over Plot

ALTERNATIVE APPROACHES TO BOOK-BUILDING

> *The book is an extension of memory and imagination.*
>
> —conversations with Jorge Luis Borges

I didn't know I *had to have* a pink toilet until I saw the one in the house of my friends Rob and Gina in the Mojave Desert. Now when I imagine my ideal house or dream dwelling, which I may never own or live in, I think first of the pink toilet, because it communicates the mood and atmosphere that feels right to me, and how or why that is I don't know, which makes it fun. Colorful bathrooms are fun? Pink is my favorite color? My best apartment in Los Angeles had a pink-tiled bathroom? Maybe all or some of that, but it was the way I reacted to this singular object that helped me begin to picture an overall vibe, tethering it to a future house, which would be tethered to the world, and I had a place in both. I didn't look at a house and think, *Wow look at the studs on that one*, or *Wow, great work with plywood*, or *Yay, mid-century and a pool too!* No. It started with a pink toilet.

The point is this: Our imagination doesn't work from the ground up, or in a linear fashion, or even from sources we fully understand; we are always hauling up memories and images from our subconscious, so why should building a book be any different? If a book is a metaphorical house, why not go big with your imagination or start small in your process of imagining it?

Just after Hurricane Andrew in 1992, I traveled to South Florida with Habitat for Humanity to help rebuild houses and distribute supplies. Alongside my well-meaning college friends, who drove from Minnesota to Florida in a smelly van, I was ready to hammer, lift, and labor. However, while the other kids were laboring on the roof or lifting things inside the house, I was left to paint because everyone was terrified to let the disabled girl climb a ladder, even though I was an athlete. I was so pissed off. I used to chop wood with my dad, work on a farm, and haul things around, and I was a legitimately expert skier, flinging myself down slopes at high speeds and traversing moguls. I was "forbidden," as our team captain said, and so I concentrated on simply doing my part, my feet on the ground, painting. After a while, I didn't mind; first, this trip was not about me getting on a ladder, or me feeling a part of something, although I did feel part of something, but it was not really about me at all. Once I got over myself, I imagined the family or couple that might be sitting in this house, painted this color, and the color became the focus of my efforts. I remember this when I'm struggling with the structure of a piece—it's not as much about the structure as it is about the way it looks and feels, and who you imagined living in it. I go back to my dependable strategies: the Five Moments of Rupture exercise, the lessons objects can teach us and how they help us access memories, the Big-Ass Document, the Sticky Note Layer Cake, and others I've discussed, which are discussed in the appendix of this book, together with a bonus playlist and some exercises.

Structure is a crucial topic, because right after *Am I a good writer?* the second most frequently question I get asked by students is *How do I structure my book? Where do I start, and how do I know if I'm on the right track? How do I organize it? I want to do the thing, but I have no idea how to begin or end the thing, please help.*

Short answer: You don't know. Yet. Also *organize* might be the wrong word.

Longer answer: It's about sharpening your intuition, or the lens through which you absorb and understand the world. An easy way to do this is to pick an image or a shape for your project, book, chapter, song. Or, as my friend and writer and fellow bereaved mother Liz Morris once said in a workshop: one of the most satisfying feeling states to be in while creating is when the writer is "living close to intuition." Writing intuitively means turning over a memory, working with an image, and this brings with it a set of strings tied to the memories that live within, behind, and all around you. The image is in your string, a kind of "fishing for memory" rod made of cobwebs, rope, chair legs, whatever.

What to begin with? is a better question than leaping straight to organizational concerns. Imagining the objects and the elements before the scaffolding is an alternative approach that can work, and it's more fun than making outlines. Find a starter image, an orienting initial shape, a "star to shoot for," as my teacher David Bradley liked to say. An intellectual and creative scaffolding can be robust one day, and the next day be easily disassembled, deconstructed, kicked over, reshaped, and reimagined. When I say to choose or think of a shape, I mean use the first shape that appears in your mind when you ask the question *What shape is this project?* Like moments in the Five Moments of Rupture exercise, the first shape to fall out of your mind is the one you follow and trust, even if it feels strange or bizarre. Your creative brain is trying to tell you something, although it may take a moment until you fully understand the assignment or decode that message. That's just fine.

Here are some examples. An adult student writing about the search for a child she gave up for adoption as a teenager: two parallel lines. An undergraduate student writing about her complicated family, essays with a scattering but also predictive quality and texture to the language: popcorn popper, the old-school stovetop kind. A graduate student writing about the difficulties of explaining her complicated physical symptoms to medical doctors: that gadget that was popular in the eighties, where you pressed your face into a bed of nonthreatening nails and then pulled back to see a nail-like shape of your face, not quite a mirror image, but a strangely accurate impression. These are just a few examples among many.

Identifying a specific shape requires an engagement with

constellations of meaning and helps us work with correlation and association versus strict causation or chronology or static plans or firm outlines. You don't need the floor plans of all the rooms: you're not robbing a bank. It frees up our intuition, activates playfulness, and keeps us from clamping down on *it must be this way.* Remember: the creative brain does not respond well—as in, not at all—to ultimatums. The story often arrives when the image is offered, even in an abstract way. An image is an invitation and the beginning of a dialogue, and it's helpful to treat it as such. In other words, ask questions of this shape and figure out what it's trying to tell you. Remember: your creative brain will bounce immediately if you shout at it. Be gentle, be curious, be willing to follow the road your mind is trying to pave for you.

A story, an essay, a record, a life: none of these is built on a solid foundation. Instead, a story is dynamic, an unseen and in-progress hiking trail through a forest, but also a road that can lift and turn and rise, maybe twist in an unexpected direction. A magical yet realistic road, a living, breathing, changing, evolving thing reliant on the blunt instrument of memory—that weird and shattering blur of images and sounds and smells and light. A book is a dream house, as Borges notes, one of memory and imagination, not concrete and drywall.

Historically, for thousands of years, home has had a nomadic element built into it, an in-motion quality. One early case study is the biblical Ruth, who after her husband dies chooses to stay with Naomi, her mother-in-law, saying, "Where you go, I will go; where you stay, I will stay. Your people will be my people, and your God my God." Her house is mobile, one of family and connection, loyalty and love; her home is a person, a friendship, a connection. Imagine Ruth and Naomi updated for modern times, traveling in a tricked-out motor home, traveling with everything they need, which is each other.

One summer I was walking through the lush gardens of the Villa Borghese in Rome when I stumbled upon a sculptural installation that stole my breath, literally. It was a sizzling afternoon, but the park was heaving with people wandering between the public art installations: trees that rose from the ground with painted and bedazzled trunks, as if from a child's fairy story; giant lights suggesting DANCE NOW THINK LATER with a stage to practice doing just that; a sleek metal outline of a man, hip-deep in water, arms overhead as if rising up out of a pond, the changing sky and shadowed or sunlit buildings filling the outline of his body, part of the world as it was part of him.

The piece that demanded my exquisite attention was one by the Argentinian conceptual artist Leandro Erlich, a visible manifestation of how I think a book—maybe a life—is created or constructed. Erlich works with perceptions of reality, challenging preconceived notions about what is real by trapping and holding ordinary objects in a way that changes our association with them and thus the frameworks through which we understand them. He messes with what we think we know, forces us to reconsider, look again, wonder. His pieces initiate a dialogue between what we believe and what we see, and what might be possible if you believe in magic—which, as an artist, you do. They're also magnificent and astounding and you cannot look away as your mind struggles to match the idea with how you understand the object presented to what it's doing in space.

This piece is a window suspended—floating—in air, seemingly untethered to the ground, as if a wizard's power is holding it there. The window itself looks like heavy wood with heavy shutters—robust and old-school and weathered, a place where Geppetto the woodworker might have made Pinocchio. A silver ladder, planted at an angle in the ground, is hooked to the window's thick ledge, but it, too, appears to be magnetically or mysteriously attached to the air, which must be—what, magnetized? The window has jagged edges, as if it's been ripped from the wall of a house like a puzzle piece, waiting for the rest of the house to arrive, or perhaps the rest of the house is just invisible save this window that floats high up in the air, or it's been through a war. The window is part of the world around it, but also completely set apart, out of place—for what use is a window in the world without a house, right? And how is it staying up there? What weird fantasy world ago we were in a fancy park in Rome and now: a window hangs in the air. It looks wrong, *off*, even dangerous at first and maybe even pointless. What's the point of looking through a window if you can already see right through it from where you're standing on the ground? You already know what's on the other side. The floating window also makes perfect creative sense in an imaginative way: things float and bounce all the time—or might—if we allowed them to. One of Erlich's pieces, the flying boat, is a structure on its side, oars at impossible angles; another is a house ripped out of the ground, trailing pieces of earth. All of them look ridiculously robust, and yet they also seem to be going somewhere. Where *is* the window going? What is it meant to frame? That boat looks like it weighs a gazillion pounds, so how is it perfectly still and balanced on an invisible knife-edge in space? In Erlich's work, objects we recognize and understand behave in ways we don't understand or resist believing; they float and melt in space, defying gravity and other laws of nature that say, *No, that can't happen*, while the art suggests that *anything can happen.*

The viewer's interaction is vital and what makes it art. If we'd never seen a window, we might not care, but a window brings with it so many memories and expectations that are attached to the viewer's emotional life; every observer contributes to what the art does in the world by the way in which they think about it. This process is invisible and immediate, and that is magic. A window that is not a window but is also a perfect representation of a window is another window into a real, imagined, or metaphorical place. All wonder starts with a belief in magic, a suspension of disbelief, faith, however you want to call it. One loaf feeds many, water into wine, resurrection—the Bible is full of these miracles, all just as illogical and fantastical as a floating window. The well-known writing workshop phrase "art is architecture" is not inaccurate, but sometimes art is also a hovering window between ground and sky in a park. Both are valid ways to build.

This alternative approach to building narrative dispenses with the notion of building the structure of the house first to make it solid. How often do you look in a magazine and think, *Ooh I'd like that in my dreamy house that overlooks a forest*, but you're living in a studio apartment in a big city? There's no reason to feel silly doing that; it's human and it's fun. These images can be aspirational, of course (like an infinity pool overlooking the ocean), but they can inject a sense of vitality into the process of determining your aesthetic, finding what moves you, deciding what you like (air, sun, birds calling outside the window) and what you thought you liked but don't anymore (a high-rise, a view of a city, a tiny balcony hovering over the din of traffic). Pattern over plot means decorating the rooms before you build them. Choosing the flooring before you know where the house will be. Sometimes the house goes up all at once, a burst of ideas and patterns and furniture arrangements. Sometimes you make the tile patterns of the backsplash in a kitchen on the dining room table before you put it on the wall. Sometimes you start with a toilet. Sometimes a window. Literally anything can be a door, and the thresholds can be anywhere you like; they can melt into the floor or hang from the ceiling.

A book, for all your imaginative labor, is biblical Ruth–level mobile, an ambulatory home of ideas and experiences and impressions, not unlike a house in a dream. I have a reappearing dream house; while it's always at the end of a dusty dirt road lined with modern people dressed up in old-time costumes as if at a museum of the plains or the frontier, the house itself differs wildly. Sometimes it's made of stone, with huge marble columns; other times it's a rickety old wooden house with a sagging porch, with quilts as room dividers and one room with a fishbowl where a giant orange fish lives next to an underwater lamp. Sometimes it is a house by a wild lake with a network of underground rooms, and stairs leading to various amusement parks. While the structure differs greatly, the house is always at the same end of the same road in whatever dreamland province or continent this is, and it carries with it the same dream feeling that defies "awake" language. Whatever the differences in these imagined homes, they are coming from my brain, my body, in a way over which I don't have intellectual or practical control. Although they don't necessarily lead to a story or a novel, the image they provide—a home that is constantly changing and feels more than familiar, almost fated, but without a particular narrative destination—is one that helps me understand that structure is always changing. Decide how you want a reader to feel inside the space; this consideration should lead the way, not an obsession with outlines or foundations or anything else that feels set in stone or that you try to force into being so. Allow this. Let your creative brain look through a wooden window in the sky.

Whatever the overall design of your work is now or will be tomorrow or someday, make the details—in this metaphor, the sentences—spectacular. Whether it's a simple green wallpaper or one that is writhing with green snakes on a gold background, each element of the room does its work, your work, the work you've chosen for it to do.

On a granular, sentence-by-sentence level, the writer and cultural critic David Bradley taught me many important lessons, mostly from the bar at the Continental Club in Austin while we listened to music and drank bourbon. He coded our papers in colors that indicated something (scene, exposition, interiority), but he did not tell us which color represented which thing. There was no legend, no decoder, and he offered no clues. When we'd ask what the colors meant, he'd say, "You have to figure it out." My pages were completely highlighted in *blue*. There was some pink scattered in as if someone had spilled bubblegum ice cream on a few words, but otherwise each page looked like a swimming pool.

"Why do you write?" David asked me when I showed up at his office hours, which was all the time. I liked and appreciated his gruff, no-nonsense approach, and I trusted him because he gave us criticism about our work that we didn't want to hear.

"Because I love it," I said, which was a lie.

"That's not why. Nobody *loves* writing. Maybe you want to *be* loved, and writing won't get you that, I can tell you. Try again."

"It makes me happy." Another lie, and he nailed it: I wanted to be loved.

"You look miserable."

"I guess . . ."

The silence seemed very loud.

"I guess I'm lonely." I didn't shout, but I felt like I had, and I was also on the verge of tears.

"Good. That's a start. At least it's true. Now explain to me why your characters never speak to each other but just sit around under large trees and think about farming and God. That's why everything is blue." The pink, I figured out, was action. Not a lot of that then. I still remind myself of this advice and pull characters out of their thought reveries beneath trees.

In addition to the power of going granular, David also taught me how to *think in threes.* The more specific a description, the more universally meaningful it will be. If you have a series of descriptions, try to have one or three instead of two; we like to have three, which is maybe why the Nicene Creed—a three-in-one God, Son, and the Holy Spirit—was a genius idea in A.D. 325, when the bishops at the Council of Nicaea codified it.

David also hated adverbs, the roaches of literature, and for a time I gave out adverb tickets in my classes when they were being overused and mimicked a police siren. David taught us to laugh at ourselves while also believing in the value of our work, of art. My nickname was Metaphor Mama because David teased me about the number of metaphors I packed onto a page just to show how well I could write a cool metaphor. He told us to earn our abstractions. He told us to funk it up with smell—blood, sweat, shit. He taught us how to build a world using sensory, concrete language and then read it aloud to be sure it had an element of song and a certain musicality to the lines because nobody wants to live in a world without music, rhythm, a recognizable beat. Through him I learned how to write with clarity and specificity, how to surrender to detail, how to cultivate particularity as a muscle while also having an eye toward utility. Through him I learned what a "workhorse" sentence can do, or one that maximizes its utility and interest. A description of water (I had a lot of these on my swimming pool–blue pages) is not interesting unless it is beach water overflowing the moat of a child's sandcastle, and then it feels miraculous. The same water might be treacherous if it's pulling the child out to sea. But water on its own, not so much. He taught me that if you're alive to your senses, you're paying attention, and a writer needs to pay exquisite attention, cultivate a sacred gaze under which everything has potential meaning in purpose. And then in the work, surrender to detail, build patterns, create and then fulfill expectations.

In the rogue, noncanonical Gospel of Thomas from the Nag Hammadi scriptures, the late first-century Gnostic source texts for the Synoptic Gospels, we meet a tough-love version of Jesus's teachings: "The work of the eyes is done. Go now and do the heart-work on the images imprisoned within you." This is part of sharpening the lens through which you invite readers to experience the world you've created, decorated, adorned. Remember: no observation is neutral and the lens or medium through which we experience the world could be through our sight or sound or touch or even taste. Our experiences vary as our embodiments differ. The lens is fluid, it's a portal, you can pass through it in whatever way you are able.

In this metaphorical approach to book-building, maybe you don't put the floor down first; instead, you might pick out the wallpaper and buy an expensive mattress and leave the frame for later. Maybe you have a roof floating in the air, maybe it's a gold dome, maybe it's thatch. Maybe you begin with an underground bunker. Maybe a Billy Haines chair sitting alone in a field. In each case, the goal is to recognize patterns over plot. The Five Moments of Rupture exercise helps with that, as it allows you to throw out tethers—like a fishing pole—to images and memories in your unconscious mind that, at that moment, want to come forward. It follows that they want to come forward for a reason, and you will likely start to see a pattern (versus an outline—those have never worked for me). This next step requires what the Greeks call διάκρισις, or *diakrisis*: discernment. That's when you go granular, read your work aloud, share it, move it around, throw it up in the air, and *play.*

Book-building is not so much a strategy, then, or a prescriptive set of *do this, then do that*, but a state of mind and a quality of energetics, and if you treat it as such, you are more likely to avoid clichés, which are narrative tantrums. Give your book a shape while you're working on it and know that—while an abstraction—imagining a shape may help you on a concrete level. Every book has a shape: open hands in the form of prayer, a boat, interlinked circles, a square, a ruin with an intact fireplace. Held in peace, fear, as an offering, held in violence, held in flux, held in power. Finding the right container. A boat, a banana, a braid. The same is true for chapter titles. Some of mine, discarded or kept, include "The Wingbeats of Insects and Birds," "The Accidental World," "Surviving the Body."

Building a book or a story or a piece this way requires leading with feelings, which means leaving room for the reader. How do you want the reader to feel in your house, or at the beginning? What is the first door they walk through like, the beginning of the experience? Just as in hospice care, when people are dying, Frank Ostaseski would say that our job is simply to hold space, *not* to freak out, but rather to be still and hold the energetic container of experience to the best of your ability. In the same way, respect the reader by holding the narrative space—albeit loosely, so people can move around.

Immersive beginnings are just that—immersive. They can be violent, soft, chaotic, or calm. How do you want the reader to feel? What scene might evoke this feeling? Open endings ensure that your reader is not left in the lurch. Closing the door intentionally but leaving a gap—the closing is temporary, not finite, ending the conversation between reader and writer *for now*, but not forever. It's like the book you reread every year or the movie you've seen over a hundred times: you're always a little bit sad when it ends, because you don't want it to end, and it's almost as if it doesn't—your imagination carries the container of the story out into the world, to other people and places, into other homes.

We are worth more than tidy story arcs or houses that don't feel extraordinary to us, or dwellings that don't bring us joy and peace or invite our exquisite attention. Our bodies, our lives, and the art we make in and through them are full of fascination and delight. Our characters and stories and paintings and songs should reflect this wonder, shine their particular light, start their unique conversations in the world.

— 11 —

Exquisite Creatures

WHAT WE TALK ABOUT WHEN WE TALK ABOUT DISABILITY

> I think that with very important things we do not overcome our obstacles. We look at them fixedly for as long as is necessary until, if they are due to the powers of illusion, they disappear.
>
> —Simone Weil, from her letters

Years ago, in high school, at a church conference in Dallas, I was in an elevator at a shitty Hyatt when the other person in the elevator—a man—gestured to my prosthetic limb and asked me, "Hey, does it go all the way up?"

"Hi, I'm Emily," I said, annoyed but unsurprised. I was wearing shorts, and if you are someone who has a visible disability *sometimes* (in shorts) and *sometimes not* (in a long dress), then your experience in the world varies wildly depending on your sartorial choices for the day. "I lost my leg when I was four."

"Do you shower with it on?" the man asked.

"Sorry, what?"

"And also, just wondering if the carpet matches the drapes."

"You mean, my hair?"

"Yes." He *winked at me.* "Redheads totally fascinate me."

"Umm, I'm here with a church group." This, of course, was not an answer to anything but was the only thing I could think of to say, and it shut him up. He scurried off on the next floor, leaving me to ascend in the glass elevator to my room that smelled like a pukey combination of cigarette smoke and rose-scented air freshener.

I have been assked these questions hundreds of times in my life, but I only remember this one time when I was asked several back-to-back in rapid-fire rudeness and by the same creepy asker. I felt so gross—as if I'd been displayed at a nineteenth-century freak show—that in my room I immediately took a shower and put on a long dress and closed-toe shoes. I longed to be completely invisible. I didn't tell anyone because I didn't want to hear the platitudes about how God loved me or whatever, how people were close-minded, etc. I believed both at the time, but I just felt tired. I wished I'd said something, but what? I didn't know shit about reclaiming my narrative or even what those words meant when pushed together. I was also taught to be nice to everyone, and I'd already spent and would continue to spend countless hours in flimsy gowns being sized up by surgeons, prosthetists, and residents in training looking at my body as if it were a medical problem to be solved. I didn't think I had a right to insist on privacy—why would I, since I'd never had any? To have a disability is to be constantly watched and watchful.

Many accusations are leveled at memoir: that it's self-centered and navel-gazing. For me, it is a privacy firewall—in fact, the only privacy I've ever experienced. In and through it, I control the narrative, me alone. I exclude what is only for me, and I include only what serves the story. My wall is carefully curated, made of bricks on fire, and nobody but me knows how to scale it because I built it and remain inside my fortress, calm and content. But this knowledge—this practice—was years away during my stay at the shitty Hyatt with my Jesus friends.

It is interesting to me that disabled people—or "mutants" as they are called in superhero movies like the *X-Men* franchise, or those with "cosmically compromised DNA" in the slightly more woke reboot of *The Fantastic Four*—are often only given full narrative agency in superhero movies. In other movies, they are often used as a foil or a tragedy, or the villain, like the one-armed man in *The Fugitive* movie. (There's a picture of Harrison Ford holding a prosthetic arm in the fitting room at my leg guy's office, and I'm told it was actually an accurate-looking arm for the time, so at least there's that.) Or disability is the worst thing that's ever happened to them and they're in misery, or else they "overcome" their disabilities through some miraculous combination of brute strength and exceptional character. But in superhero movies, nonnormative people are given backstories and motivations, real relationships and real things to do, and they're also not always at ease with the abilities of their unique bodies, and they're not always shining examples of morally superior Tiny Tim–like people. They must adapt to their bodies that are both magnificent and mundane, and adapt to the way the world views them, the second sometimes being the biggest lift, and sometimes doing all this makes them angry, bitter, and violent.

Being different is exhausting, even when someone isn't trying to actively kill you, like Galactus in *The Fantastic Four*—a giant AI thing meets the *Ghostbusters* Marshmallow Man meets Sauron meets the mean Terminator trying to kill the nice Terminator. There's a fine line between curiosity and revulsion—this drives part of the tension in many superhero blockbusters—and is well known to anyone who lives with a disability. So, too, is the pervasive use of words as metaphor that are dismissive and inaccurate: paralyzed with fright (only you weren't paralyzed; you were having a flight response and couldn't move), spastic, retarded, lame, crippled, crippling, the list goes on.

In *The Fantastic Four*, Galactus of the nightmare-level-scary voice has decided that he will only spare planet Earth if Reed Richards (Mr. Fantastic) and Sue Storm (Invisible Woman), a superhero power couple who went into space and became super bendy and able to disappear and storm people out of the way, respectively, give him their unborn son, Franklin, who may or may not have "cosmically compromised DNA." Before they head off, Reed makes a promise to Franklin: "The unknown will become known, and we will protect you." The Fantastic Four fly away to fight this new threat, and come to face to face with the Devourer of Worlds.

Galactus offers them a choice: the world will be spared if Franklin is sacrificed. This is not a choice, of course, not even for two people charged with protecting the world from nasty entities hell-bent on ushering in death and doom. This is their *child*. Franklin will not be eaten by this horrible monster, *and* the world will be saved from annihilation. And because Susan and Reed are superheroes, they just might make it happen. Galactus has an idea, however. "I will spare your world. In exchange for the boy," he booms. Sue holds her womb as if she can protect her unborn child. Reed is just as incapable in that moment of saving his son but is more certain of his ability to do so (he's a man, after all, and he's literally called Mr. *Fantastic*): "You will not have our planet," he shouts up at the big metal monster with glowing eyes. "And you will not have our son!"

They spirit back to Earth just in time, but they've been warned by Galactus that "I will eat your planet slowly while your child watches." Later, Reed tells the press conference convened to update the people of Earth about their possible impending demise that nobody is safe, and that he isn't sure what to do. Reed: "He said, 'Give us your child, and I will spare the earth.' We said no, obviously. We said no." This doesn't go over so well, and it takes Sue holding Franklin, the baby, to get the world to come together. She is a woman with superhero powers and she still must do the very normal emotional labor of all women to get the grumpy, frightened mob on board. Johnny (the Human Torch) and Ben (the Thing) are appalled but don't know what to do; it's not their kid, although they would risk their lives to protect him.

This is what I love most about superhero movies: they are so epic, so intentionally melodramatic, so full of dopey comedic guffaws, full of special effects and explosions that are distracting and entertaining, of course, but when seen through a particular lens of experience, they are quite deep. I know this because the first time I watched *X-Men: First Class*, a year before Ronan died, I was in a state of such active despair that I sobbed through the whole movie. I would have done the same in *The Fantastic Four* had it been released during my son's life, only my lens has shifted over this decade, and with it, my emotional response to and with all art, even the action movie kind.

I watched *X-Men: First Class* in 2012, when Ronan was still alive but had hit the downward spiral that would eventually end in his death. In the opening sequence, a young boy, Erik, is asked to move a coin across a table before the count of three or his mother will be shot. It is Poland, 1944, and Erik's mother, emaciated and terrified, tries to calm her son as he attempts to save her life. The ruthless Sebastian Shaw begins the countdown. Erik concentrates, fingers trembling, watching the gun, then the unmoving coin, glancing over his shoulder at his mother, who tries in vain to reassure him ("Everything is okay," she repeats, mother to the last, knowing that they'll both lose this battle). Erik tries desperately to use an extraordinary gift that the Nazis discovered during the liquidation of the Jewish ghetto, when out of fear and desperation he bent an iron gate as his parents were being dragged away. He cannot do it; the stress is too great. He fails the test, and Shaw shoots his mother in the heart.

This unleashes Erik's power. In that fuselage of pain and rage and sadness, screaming, crying, he lifts his thin hands: lamps break into pieces and metal helmets compress the heads of the guards standing over his dead mother. He spins objects wildly around the office and the "experiment" room, full of metal probes and leather straps and other shining instruments of torture that Shaw has used to try to manipulate Erik's abilities, culminating in this final test. Shaw, however, is thrilled to see the havoc his protégé is capable of when pushed to the edge, and he slips the coin into Erik's hand and happily observes that pain and anger will "unlock his gift." He might have instead said a single word to explain such a violent, full-body feeling that is pain + anger + tortured sadness = grief. In that moment Magneto—a man distrustful of a world that wants to squash difference, manipulate it, abuse it, and destroy it, wherever it might manifest itself—the man Erik becomes, is born.

If theology is a fusion of history, literature, and philosophy, then grief is the fusion of sadness, rage, and helplessness. I saw this, at the time, as a manifestation of a powerful truth about grief: that it fucks things up, and not just inanimate objects like chairs and tables and tools, but people too. Their hearts. It, quite literally, *ruins*. Feeling as though I'd been punched in the gut, I cried for the next hour and a half. I kept seeing that boy screaming "No," a primal, grief-stricken howl, as he makes chairs clash together and metal crumple and knives fly while his mother is lying on the ground behind him: dead, shot, gone. I felt like I knew, in some way, what Erik/Magneto was about, just as

I understood what Sue was about when she refused to give up her kid, even if to do so would mean saving the world. (Interestingly enough, Pedro Pascal, the actor who portrays Reed, plays a character who does something similar in *The Last of Us.* In one powerful scene, full of rage and determination and sheer will, he anchors what felt to me like the most accurate and devastating depiction of what a parent would do for their child, which is to kill everyone who is trying to kill her, even though the child's death—the parts of her DNA that make her immune to a lethal virus that is destroying the world—could save *everyone.* It's one of the most terrifying and true scenes about grief that I have ever watched on television. There is no sound. Pascal embodies a silent howl of single-minded rage. He is going to save his girl, no matter the cost to others.) The moral nuance of both of these action movies is made even more complicated and interesting when seen through the thought prism of the odd and brilliant Simone Weil, who blazed a brave moral path all her own before her death at the age of thirty-four, and who observed, in her essay "The Love of God and Affliction," that "at the very best, he who is branded by affliction will only keep half his soul." We see Erik struggle to keep that half intact for the rest of the film.

This installment of *X-Men* set the stage for future epic conflicts between Magneto and Professor X, so there are plenty of exploding buildings and special effects, but beneath that the film offers some deep meditations on difference, on ability, on friendship, on what it feels like to be labeled and set apart. The characters reveal ways in which our outsider experiences, our early wounds, do not disappear; in fact, they never leave us. The residue from these narratives impacts our moral choices to the point of altering our understanding of what choices we actually *have*, and sometimes even ferreting this out is a struggle. Weil again: "As for those who have been struck by one of those blows which leave a being struggling on the ground like a half-crushed worm, they have no words to express what is happening to them." In other words, definitions of *moral universe* are as diverse as ladders of DNA. It's hard to think clearly when someone is trying to crush you under the many systems that seek to do so: racism, sexism, ableism, homophobia, patriarchy, and the way these systems support and strengthen and uphold patterns of abuse. These systems are like umbrella terms that we talk about as abstractions and isms but are major engines of plot. Your decisions are not always wholly your own; umbrellas matter, because if you have to stand under one or more, it determines how and when and where you can act. In *The Fantastic Four*, the four astronauts who were altered in their cosmic journeys are relatively subdued. They don't have basement caves full of luxury cars that fly or long-suffering butlers like Bruce Wayne; they don't have day jobs as a journalist like Superman; they don't have crushes on girls at school like Spiderman. They have serious science jobs, diplomatic jobs; they are on the world stage. They also go to markets and buy cookies, they are out and about, they have spaghetti dinners every Sunday night. They're like the cast of *Friends*, only with special powers and more interesting conversations.

Only in superhero movies does a nonnormative body

make you happily extraordinary, gifted with enviable if misunderstood powers. My experiences were quite different: The first time I stripped down to my underwear in front of medical residents at the children's hospital so they could examine, precisely, the way my artificial leg fit against my hip as I trotted down the hallway in my open-back robe, I was six. My parents and I went for pizza afterward, but I had lost my appetite. My congenital deformity, my fluke, my genetic mutation, my crappy luck, made me an interesting specimen, an object for medical inquiry. I was not a girl, or even a person, but a thing, and, by medical definition, an unfortunate, abnormal one. I understood, in an unspoken way, that the body was a problem and, in this case at least, it could only be partially solved.

Thirty years later, I thought I'd purged all my discussions of disability when the eye doctor saw the cherry-red spots at the back of Ronan's retinas, the definitive marker of the disease, a disease I was tested for, even though, as the genetic counselor at Cedars-Sinai Medical Center in Los Angeles said, "You don't need it; you don't look Jewish." "I was tested, I was tested," I screamed at the eye doctor, wailing, crumpling, pissing my pants, feeling, in no uncertain terms *the void, the void*, but it turns out that the prenatal test only detects nine "common" mutations, not all hundred plus. I didn't have Mr. Fantastic to test every possible combination or probability of disaster, but I did have the confidence to say what Sue Storm does when Reed gets worried: "He's normal . . . There's nothing wrong with him." All along I thought the problem was physical, not internal, that what made *me* different could not be passed down. I was wrong. For the short duration of his life, Ronan did the rounds of neurologists and geneticists and specialists who looked at him the way doctors once looked at me: This baby is different, of a different kind. Not one of us. White: check. But able: no check. Normal: no check. Someone with a future: no check.

Once, while I was being patted down by a TSA agent in an American airport, he said, "I've never seen one like you before." During a "private screening" at an obscure African airport, I was asked to remove my pants as, one by one, the security agents touched my leg, quickly, with just the tip of a finger, as if they might get an electric shock (if only!). Only one doctor in New Mexico had seen a Tay-Sachs baby before Ronan. I would not have been surprised if one morning when I plucked Ronan from his crib he would have sprouted a horn from the middle of his head, wings from his back, maybe a tail. That would have been fine with me, because he was magical.

While the characters of *The Fantastic Four* are more or less all happy about the gifts granted them by their powers (apart from the Thing, who is now a giant rock person, while his friends remain outwardly normal and as hot as they always were). In *X-Men: First Class*, we see a boy wake in the middle of the night to find a blue girl disguised as his mother foraging for food in his kitchen. This young telepath reads her mind and politely extends his hand, promising, "You never have to be alone again." This is Charles Xavier; optimistic and wealthy, he grows up to be a renowned Oxford-educated professor—Professor X. A brilliant expert on genetic mutation, Charles chats up girls in pubs with pickup lines like "Your mutation is groovy." He can read minds, influence actions, and even erase memories, but he looks "normal," and he is a white man, and has every privilege afforded him as he moves freely through the world, passing as nonmutant. The blue girl, Raven, becomes his sidekick, masquerading as a coed hottie with a cherubic face and blond hair. Charles believes in assimilation, in mutants and humans living together. He is mutant and proud, but he also doesn't want to rock the boat too much. When Raven changes her eye color in a bar, he promptly drags her back to their damp flat, where he announces that he must study. Why should he reject the world? Why not find a way to live in it? The boat has always worked in his favor, sailing him to happy shores and a very comfortable if slightly complicated life.

But there's a toughness to Charles. He risks his life for other mutants, working always toward his idea of goodness, which is the group. He meets Erik for the first time when he dives into the ocean to save him and tells Erik (with his mind), "Come with us, you are one of us, you are not the only one." Erik is shocked and surprised; all this time he thought he was an island far from any shore, isolated. Now he hears a voice: "Do not despair. You are one of us."

When I was in the seventh grade, I went on a ski trip with a group of kids from the local evangelical church. Although at the time I would not have been able to articulate that my values or theological views differed (as in, they were the opposite) from these twenty-odd people who prayed in circles, shouted in church (I grew up Lutheran; we did not shout, ever), and began sentences with the very missionary-friendly statement *We know these things are true* before reciting a biblical passage with slightly glazed-over eyes, I did still believe in Jesus, and I believed even more in the delights of skiing, which is how I ended up on the trip.

One night before the predinner prayer circle, I stood in a group of nervous, giggling girls in our youth pastor's motel room. Let's call him Jeremy. He sat in the wooden chair that he'd pulled away from the rickety desk in the corner of the budget motel room (ever the morbid one, I thought of a chair one would stand on in a room as lonely as this in order to hang oneself, but I kept this to myself), and he was lecturing us about sex. Or basically, why we should, under no circumstances, be having it or even thinking about it, although there were some things he needed to tell us, so he'd deliberately gathered us all together in order to bring it (sex, that is) up. Snow tumbled past the windows—sharp flakes, and less than I'd hoped; the runs were rocky and icy, no powder at all. The heater hissed in the corner and the room was uncomfortably warm. As I stood in a line facing Jeremy and his words (a single-man morality firing squad), I wished I could walk to the other side of the room and press my forehead against the cold window pane. DON'T HAVE SEX UNTIL YOU ARE MARRIED, he warned (and then, I guess, don't enjoy it, but he certainly didn't say that). We'd heard this before: from our parents, from our teachers, from our well-meaning friends—the purity/promise bracelets were just getting started in small-town Nebraska in the late eighties—but Jeremy decided to make a point. He stood up from his chair. Boy crazy and awestruck as we were by this man with the strong jaw and the broad shoulders and the college girlfriend who was *still*, he told us proudly, *a virgin*, we fell silent. Snow continued falling past the window. A cleaning cart rattled past the doorway along the concrete pathway outside, and a woman shouted, "Mañana!" Nobody said a word. Without taking his eyes from our group, he gestured at the chair behind him.

"This chair is a symbol," he intoned in his practiced, preacherly voice. "When my wife and I *make love* for the first time . . ." He had to stop for a moment for the giggles, which he silenced with a meaningful glare. "I'll put a chair near the bed and say, 'This is for Jesus. We waited like good Christians, and he's here to consecrate our love.'"

"Conse-what?" someone said. She was elbowed in the ribs by her neighbor.

Today's hip teenagers might make jokes about the silly chair ("Jesus likes to watch?"), but we girls from farm towns and religious, painfully old-fashioned families weren't experienced enough to make that joke, and the odd sexualization of teenagers hadn't yet permeated television and movies; and the internet, with all its pathways to pornography and other naughtiness, did not yet exist.

We waited obediently. "Okay, you can go," he said, but as we filed out, he asked me to stay back for a moment. He waited for the last girl to leave; the door clicked shut behind her. I watched a bead of sweat on his forehead slip behind his ear. My right thigh hurt from skiing; my shoulders ached from gripping the outriggers, small skis attached to metal poles that clamped around my upper arms and allowed me to ski on one leg.

"Emily, I need to tell you something," he said. I was sure he was going to confess his undying love for me, a feeling made more complicated by the fact that he smelled like my dad's cologne, which eliminated him as an object of desire. Plus, I thought he was dumb, which was a major turnoff.

"My advice may not apply to you," he said. My heart dropped into my stomach. *Oh. My. God.* Was he propositioning me for sex? Was he one of those predatorial teacher-priest types I'd been warned about my whole young life but—at least to my knowledge—had never met? If so, I knew exactly what to do: scream, get away, tell a parent or another trusted adult. Or was he getting ready to consecrate something not with his sanctimonious girlfriend but with me?

"People don't," he began, looking past me toward the window. I looked with him. Someone wearing a red coat was sprinting through the snow. It was late afternoon, the sun was disappearing, and the sky was twilight blue, the color of change and possibility. "Men . . . uh . . . boys . . . will have a difficult time with . . . with difference. So, you shouldn't worry about what I just told you." He stood up and put his hand on my shoulder. "You just live your life."

Which, apparently, meant a sexless one. Nobody would want to have sex with me. I wasn't initially concerned—it was first-kiss drama and the upcoming prom that loomed largest—but later, after yet another boring prayer circle and tasteless dinner and then lights out, I couldn't sleep.

Everyone knew about the artificial leg—I skied without it—but now I understood that there were larger ramifications for the rest of my life, including my sex life, which I envisioned less as a life than a vague notion that terrified me but that I understood was linked to activities experienced by people who loved and desired one another, although desire was never a part of religious discussions about sex. We were told to desire God, to desire goodness and righteousness, without having the notion of desire unpacked in any way, and with goodness being defined solely as the other side of evil with no room for an impulse that might lie somewhere in the murky and unidentified middle. I lay under the covers feeling stripped, bare and exposed, in all my difference. In all my freakishness and deformity. Alone. One thing that still comforts me about Ronan is that he never lay alone in bed, feeling like a freak. He sat on my lap and smiled and played with the toys I held out to him and did not care about others' opinions of him, including mine. If it didn't cost him his life, he would have been a model of confidence.

The Fantastic Four are pressed into service to the planet. They confidently stop evil baddies and live in mid-century houses with a cool little robot who, like R2-D2, can only be understood through the tone of his voice and context clues. They are united in the world, or at least they think they are until a weird silver woman on a surfboard swoops into their lives and tells them they're all about to die.

In *X-Men*, the CIA recruits Erik and Charles to fight for America, and using Charles's telepathic powers, they convince others like them to join the world-saving fun. In one scene, the new mutant recruits, all with various powers, sit in a room and show off. It's the first time they've been able to reveal what makes them special: wings; the ability to spit fire; hands where the feet should be; a blue body that can take the shape of anyone else's; an ability to adapt to any environment, even growing gills underwater spontaneously. "Watch this," they say euphorically in turn, and everybody cheers at what they can do. They feel evolved in this moment, special in the best sense. The moment sours when several CIA agents jeer at them through the window glass like ticket holders at a freak show, demanding to be wowed. (Rosemarie Garland Thomson wrote an amazing book of literary theory called *Extraordinary Bodies* that breaks down the sociopolitical aspects of the nineteenth-century freak show and dissects the treatment of disability in literature from Dickens to DeLillo.) Walking with my student and friend in her wheelchair to the Culver Hotel in Los Angeles for an event several years ago, a group of people passed us and one of them said, out loud, as if we could not hear them or see that they were staring, "What is it, the freak convention?" That we heard it together didn't make it any better to bear. As the dopey CIA guys shuffle off, the winged, fire-spitting girl who once worked as a stripper says she'd rather be stared at with her clothes off instead of the way those men, leering, through the window, had looked at her. In *The Fantastic Four*, our superpowered astronauts are heroes, the defenders of the realm, lauded and beloved. Until they aren't.

At mutant summer camp, under Charles's patient and

faithful tutelage, the kids learn to control their powers, to embody their differences and help the CIA to further its goals of fostering goodness and maintaining life as everyone knows it. Our fab four don't go through a painful process of acceptance, because the world is out to love them—until it isn't.

The characters in these two movies have different kinds of narrative agency. While the X-Men were "born this way," in much the same way as Frankenstein's monster, the Fantastic Four made a choice to go up into space, and luckily for them, their mutant powers were acceptable because they were protective and with the exception, again, of the Thing, they mostly looked normal until they were asked to fight evil and then they just looked cool. Up until his meeting with Charles, Erik has been on a globe-trotting quest for revenge. "Who are you?" the bartender asks after Erik kills two Germans living in Argentina, who, when they see Erik's tattoo, explain that they were just following orders. "Just think of me as Frankenstein's monster, here to find my creator," Erik responds, glancing at a photograph of Shaw, the man he's looking for, mounted on the wall. There's nothing I love more than a reference to Mary Shelley's book in a comic book movie—the perfect synthesis of absurdity and profundity.

All along, Erik aims to kill his creator, although Charles warns him that such an action will not bring him peace, which, according to Erik, was never an option. He's gunning for Shaw because he is compelled, even morally obliged to do so; he is obeying some inner voice that says, *Destroy the man who killed your mother,* and he cannot say that this path isn't right. Simone Weil described faith as a kind of descent, a necessary obedience to gravity, an inevitable drop, a loosening and a giving in. Erik is dropping down from the first frame of the film. Reed and Sue refuse to sacrifice their son to the vile need of a destructive villain, although from an ethical perspective, they probably should—one life for many. Morally, however, they will do no such thing, as this would be violating their primal oaths as parents, the first job of which is to protect their child.

In *X-Men,* Charles is training mutants to serve the world, but Erik is doing some recruiting of his own. "You want to be accepted," he tells Raven, who doesn't want to show her true blue color because she's ashamed, "but you can't even accept yourself." In the end, Raven chooses Fassbender instead of her other crush, who has developed a serum (faulty, as it turns out) that he promises will preserve her powers but make her normal according to acceptable standards of beauty and, as he says in one wrenching scene, "truly beautiful." Erik, on the other hand, says, "I want to see the real Raven," and when, lying in his bed, she flutters into her full-on blue glory, he lies next to her, touches her face, and kisses her, saying, "You are an exquisite creature." This might be a comic book movie, but to me this is one of the most romantic things a man has ever uttered to a woman on-screen. Right behind this is Reed weeping over Sue after she uses up her powers.

When I was pregnant, I felt redeemed, suddenly plucked from the mutant group and plopped into a far less (I thought) complicated group. I've always been asked to tell the story of my body in public by nosy strangers, but now the questions, which seemed at the time, less menacing, were "How far along?" and "When are you due?" instead of "What happened to you?" or "Why are you limping?" I got pregnant quickly, and everything progressed "normally." My body was doing what women's bodies were meant to do, and it seemed to be doing it easily. Each ultrasound was fine, the fluid around the baby was fine. I was cycling and doing yoga, and the baby was growing, and I could hardly believe how good it felt, how easy it was, how pretty I looked. My hair was long and lush, and my skin was soft. I had been expecting catastrophe and here was this physical bliss. When we received the early amniocentesis results, the doctor said, "It couldn't look any better." And yet "You won't give him *that*? Will you?" one man asked me, entirely unprovoked and without preliminaries, at a Los Angeles Whole Foods, pointing first to my leg (I was wearing a short skirt) and then at my belly. This time I refused to answer. When Ronan was born, I kept thinking of the story I told so many people: When did that happen? How long? When? Why? *At birth. From birth. Because of birth.*

There's a scene in *The Fantastic Four* where Reed (played by everyone's favorite daddy, Pedro Pascal) is performing an ultrasound on his son. Sue Storm (the ridiculously luminous Vanessa Kirby) reminds her nerdy science genius of a husband that they did all the tests, and there was "nothing wrong" with their child; he was "fine." Perfectly normal. Thirteen years earlier, I would have sobbed during that scene. But my interpretive lens has changed with time and with it, my grief, and so I simply noted how I responded to it, how it resonated, without descending into tears.

There are so many narratives folded into this movie: the only-son, Messiah-like figure (Jesus) whom Galactus insists the parents must sacrifice (Isaac), only Reed and Sue are no Joseph and Mary, they do not agree with this; they are no Abraham and Sarah; they may bait Galactus with their son, Franklin, but they will find a way to save him, or die trying. In fact, Sue *literally dies trying*, using all her power to shove asshole Galactus into a vortex before he can cart away her baby, with help from the silver woman on the surfboard who has her own complicated backstory and decides to sacrifice herself for the good of the world she had only weeks ago chosen to destroy in service of Galactus.

In the scene when Franklin is placed on Sue's chest, this baby, who is somehow an amazing actor, is actually abnormal too, but in the best way. Turns out, he is a healer. He's not evil at all; in fact, he is godlike, benevolent and gifted. He raises his mother from the dead. He is an only son. A devilish figure who calls himself the DEVOURER is trying to destroy him. Remind you of anyone else's dilemmas or capabilities? In the healing narratives of the Synoptic Gospels, Jesus heals a man who is then lifted out of a roof, and he can suddenly walk when he could not before; a woman brushes against Jesus in a crowd and is healed. Perfect Pedro (marry me) is weeping over his beloved wife, who sacrificed herself for her magical baby son, but only in that moment can the baby reveal his powers (turns out he is also a super genius, and a few years later is able to read and understand *The Origin of Species* in a matter of days). The healing narratives are problematic for people with disabilities, as they are often used as metaphors for the ways in which Jesus makes us "whole" by "removing the sin" that created the anomaly in the first place. But Franklin's anomaly can't be detected, although Reed has tested for all of them, because it's invisible. And it's not fatal or evil; it's love. This is a nice touch. The gift of salvific love cannot be detected on an ultrasound, but only in and through human connection, the primal bond of mother-child love. Earlier in the movie, after Galactus demands to have the baby or he'll ruin the earth, Sue insists that while her boy may have powers she doesn't yet know or understand, she will not give up her son. That would have made me cry a decade ago; now, it just made me happy, and I thought, *That's what parenting is. Good job, movie people.*

The final sequence of *X-Men* is a bit more intense. Erik confronts Shaw. Before he strikes the lethal blow, he hangs, balanced, in a delicate equilibrium of rage and love. In the end, however, he cannot have both, and he chooses to kill Shaw, rejecting mercy. Although I think audiences are supposed to believe that Erik loses his moral center when he becomes the monster his monster-creator had intended him to be, it's not that simple. It's not the choice we're supposed to like, this rejection of Charles's "we the mutants" slogan, but I would argue that it's not necessarily immoral. Weil, although she liked parties and was actually quite sociable, was fearful of the royal *we*, fearful of the impression like minds could make on an individual, suspicious of her ability to get sucked into the collective spirit, which is why she never joined the church and spent a lot of time alone, thinking for herself, considering the world and how people moved through it. She was famous for saying that if she heard kids singing a Nazi song, then part of her would become a Nazi so she just steered clear of big groups all together. Her morality was too bendy and this frightened her. She wanted her experience of God to be pure, so isolation was the ticket for her, although this, too, was incorrect, as Weil abhorred the idea of will, and thought about faith in terms of gravity—it falls on you, you fall into it, passivity is the ultimate sacred stand when it comes to encountering (indeed, waiting) for God. Faith. As surrender. "The flesh impels us to say *me* and the devil impels us to say *us*," she writes in her letters. Magneto followed his flesh impulse, the demand that rang out from his bones. I can't say I disagree with him.

After Shaw is murdered and the nuclear threat he'd been plotting is neutralized, the CIA decides that the mutants have played their role in saving America and now it's time to get rid of these freaks for good, especially now that they've been isolated on a remote island. They launch the missiles, and as Erik is turning the missiles around, striking back, and Charles is trying to stop him—even though he's sick with the betrayal, he can hardly believe it—a stray bullet lodges in Charles's back and paralyzes him from the waist down. Erik cradles his friend, the only one he's ever known or loved, and he's sorry for the accident but he can't be sorry for his choice, and we get just enough pathos from Charles, saying, stoically but fearfully, "I can't feel my legs I can't feel my legs," the world literally snatched beneath him, blaming his friend but unable, even now, to stop loving him. The two friends step into different voids and from now on they will be enemies without sacrificing the love they bear for one another. I understood Magneto's decision to meet rejection with rejection. When Ronan was dying, I felt like I could bring a plane down with my grief or wipe out a planet, or, like Sue Storm, beat back the force that was trying to take my kid with so much power it would kill me. I understand his desire for retaliation. I do not think he is wrong. As it turns out, Jeremy, the minister from the church group, presented a far less nuanced moral view than what's offered in *The Fantastic Four* or *X-Men*. He offered platitudes in place of faith, a regurgitated set of beliefs rather than honest wrangling with what it means to be faithful, human, *good*. The one big argument Sue and Reed have is this: that each of them thought about sacrificing their child, even though in the end they don't.

Simone Weil famously said, "affliction is ridiculous." It doesn't mean it's funny, but like a hard-hitting joke, it turns expected reactions, quite literally, around, sometimes topples them. My first encounter with Weil left me annoyed—such a ruthless aesthetic, such obsessive individuality—but rereading her work during Ronan's life, I found her refreshingly, relentlessly self-reflexive and prophetic and unafraid to articulate her core beliefs about herself, people, and the world. She interrogates and examines her thoughts, trying to be, quite simply, good. The path she chooses is not an easy one, but she refuses to resist it, and this relaxing into absolute brokenness—her true vulnerability—provides the foundation for moral activity. Virtue is meaningless, worthless—it tries too hard; it strives too ardently to make itself the object of itself. To fall into faith is to know true love: of self, of another, of the world, of God.

When Erik weeps like Frankenstein's monster over the man who destroyed and created him, he owns his choice. To reject Charles's way doesn't mean Erik doesn't love him—he does—but Erik's way, his series of choices, were forged in the fire of an experience the emotional consequences of which few of us can fully imagine or appreciate, let alone deeply understand—even Charles, the deeply empathetic telepath. Erik's morality was created solely, like Weil's, through experience. She only ever trusted her mind, not what people told her she should be, think, do. She wanted to be saved but she would not be baptized. She wanted to be alone with her experience of Christ but would join no church or religious order. She, like Erik, was set apart, different, haunted, although the haunting had very different origins.

Death, for Weil, was that one time when humans actually get it right, the only moment of unadulterated truth that a human person will ever have access to, because it IS so fleeting, and happens right before they disappear. Sue can disappear because that's one of her cool powers, and one I often wish I had in elevators: once when Reed is checking the baby again for problems with his ultrasound wand, and when Sue gives birth.

"One must believe in the reality of Time," Weil wrote in her notebooks. "Otherwise one is just dreaming." Ronan lived in a perpetual state of being-in-the-now that people make Herculean efforts to achieve. Was Ronan more evolved if we take Weil's definition of time at face value? Did he embody a Tay-Sachs baby version of nirvana, a kind of perpetual, existential bliss, or is this just trying to sprinkle glitter on a pile of shit, glossing over an absurdly tragic situation? Can it be both?

Writers are supposed to say it can be both; we're supposed to muck around in the moral gray area, bringing it to life rather than trying to explain it away. The writerly inclination (indeed, the responsibility, according to David L. Ulin in *The Lost Art of Reading*) is to stare down the abyss and then render it, but this brings with it the attendant danger of being unable to look away, of getting locked inside that darkness and eventually being unable to look for a door or even a crack of light. The writers I have always loved—Dostoevsky, Tolstoy, Porter, Baldwin, Atwood, Munro, McCullers, hooks, Ondaatje—don't accuse their "bad" characters of moral failure, but instead narrate the progress of a mind, a forward, spiral motion that sometimes leads to murder, or deception, or death, or simple laziness, or fatal perversion. But it is never depicted as a failure; amazingly, neither is Magneto's defection from goodness. Galactus, on the other hand, has zero nuance; he is just all bad, so he is not a true villain but a stereotype, and *The Fantastic Four* is easier to watch as a result. Also, Pedro Pascal is in it. At several points, he promises that he will save the world and all the people he loves. Okay. Yes, please.

Finding a new way to be in the world can be a lonely enterprise when the world turns on you or was designed to reject your body from the get-go. A reinvention of life, Weil believed, can create desperation. She wanted only to anchor herself to the truth of her experience. Plenty of people thought she was misguided, selfish, self-indulgent, ridiculous. I wanted to anchor Ronan to the world, make him known through my writing, but I understood that this would not save him. I felt compelled to try regardless. He still died. I wanted to be seen as normal, as belonging. I still do, but now I understand that I have always belonged—if not entirely to the world, then to myself and to the people I love and *for* the world I want to create.

Weil claimed a unique faith rooted in her raw experience, outside of all tradition, but without being dismissive of institutions or people who found comfort in that organized expression of religion. Suffering, for Weil, is always the moral choice; it is, in fact, the evidence of love because it provides the opportunity for the sufferer to give in, give up, and wait for God. The abyss, then, is good news, because there's nothing you can do about it but leap inside. It's a leap to love; it's a leap to create. I hope to spend the rest of my life being bold enough to do both, no matter the cost. I would change that word *suffering* to *surrender.*

Over a decade after Ronan's death, I still don't have mutant powers, but I can watch *The Fantastic Four* and not sink into a grief fugue as I did with *X-Men*. I can't bend metal or stop time, or make hex A, the singular enzyme my son needed for his survival, but I have the memory of a love that shaped me, changed me, continues to guide me. I have the lens through which I learned to understand the world and all its terrible truths and unexpected beauty, and this has melded with a new lens through which I now experience the world. These two portals of understanding have collapsed into the one. I still have my heart and my mind, and I had, for a brief time, my son, my exquisite creature, genetically flawed, a gorgeous sweet-faced mutant baby. A baby with no point of view, who existed in a constant state of present attention and nothing more, which, according to Weil, put him in a constant state of prayer, which made him perfect, which made him, according to Weil's thinking, the embodiment of love. A situation both perverse and exquisite.

Theologian Gordon D. Kaufman believed that God is a creative construct, and that creativity is God in action. I think Weil might agree; we co-create our world through our experiences, and our experience of the same world changes with the lens through which we experience it. In Kaufman's constructive theology—hopeful, collaborative, radical—we all participate in the divine act of creativity because that is why we're alive. Memoir has been, for me, the superpower that tethers me to the world, even as the world says nonnormative bodies have no place. They do, or they wouldn't exist, in Kaufman's worldview, because all bodies matter as much as the notion or idea of God. Through us, art changes with and for and within us to move out of us and into service to the world.

I am still asked irritating, vaguely sexual, predatory, and wildly inappropriate questions in elevators and the occasional bank queue, and I certainly wish to be, in those moments, the Invisible Woman. When a stranger asks me if

I shower with my leg on, I'm tempted to say, "Hey, rando, do you shower with your jeans on? Or do you just like to get them *alllllll* wet? See how weird that sounds? And I see that you are bald! Does the doorknob match the knob?" Or maybe, "Ooh, I guess I've activated your exquisite attention. I totally love it when people see how exquisite I am. All this and bionic too!" What I actually say: "Well, I've written a bunch of books about it, but as my daughter likes to say, you can search them up! Since you didn't ask, this is my name. But please think of buying from an indie bookstore."

Because I've written memoir, I understand and believe that nobody has a right to my body's narrative unless I choose to share it how, when, and where I wish. I am not being brutally honest or bleeding raw on the page or other dramatic nonsense that claims to describe a successful memoir. No. I am protecting myself, and memoir is the shield, the narrative superpower. People certainly don't have a right to ask questions about my entire embodied history without even saying hello, asking my name, or sharing theirs. "The unknown will become known," Reed Richards promises Earth's residents when he tells them he won't give up the world or his son. Well, maybe it will, maybe it won't, but I have learned to own my narrative, and to embody all the versions of myself that helped me survive, and to accept the way the lens I use to understand the world has been reshaped dramatically over the years. A lens is everyone's superpower, though just like any power that is truly powerful, it has limits. That's why Galactus isn't scary; he's too needy, too sure of his position, too fully known, too much like an embodiment of capitalism that eats worlds and people's dreams and tells them they ought to feel grateful. The Fantastic Four don't know what to do, which makes them human and believable because they are mucking around in the chaotic truth of life, a place where the unknown is perhaps more ethical than the known.

To be disabled is to be exiled; to have a terminal illness is to be isolated in one's time-limitedness; to grieve is to be annihilated; and to live is inevitable: all of these, together and at once, form the core of the truth of being human. So, too, does "the instant of death," which is "the centre and object of life . . . it is the instant when, for an infinitesimal fraction of time, pure truth, naked, certain and eternal enters the soul." Weil wants all of the world, death-in-life and life-in-death, which is why she stands so spectacularly alone in her singular understanding of God piercing her, literally, with suffering, which is also the only truth worth hanging your life on.

Epilogue

Writing as an Act of Service

You absorb a thing and then you do a thing, then you absorb that thing to do another thing, and then all these things become intertwined until heat and pressure congeal them into a sequence in your mind. The process repeats. The sequences accumulate, mingle, and interlock to form a history that can be shared, and it is through such exchanges that you realize, against all odds, you've become a person.
—Heather McCalden, from *The Observable Universe*

The summer before I went to divinity school, I worked at Barbara's Bestsellers, a kiosk at South Station in Boston. People might pick up a book to read on the train to New Haven or New York or to the Boston suburbs. Most of the time, they browsed without buying anything. Those books were like the bowls of peanuts at bars: loaded with bacteria. We were supposed to engage the customers and suggest selections. I did none of this. Instead, I sat behind the register and read books I had chosen for myself, hoping to limit my interactions with customers to the few minutes when the exchange of a book for money took place. I'd been working retail for so many years: selling camo pants and duck decoys at a sporting goods store during high school in Nebraska; then bras and khaki trousers and flannel shirts (in the *same mall*—ugh) during college holiday breaks in Colorado; then beers and hot wings at a microbrewery in Boston, which was still a relatively new concept at the time. I was over customer service and people-ing and speaking in a singsong customer service voice. I read during my shift to the comforting white noise of announced train times and departures, the click of heels or dress shoes across the floor, a ribbon of laughter or the whip of an argument rushing past. I wouldn't know someone else was even in the kiosk until they strolled up to the cash register and said hello. It was a bit like being in the hospital; I felt calm, safe, and at home inside all that ambient noise. Plus: I read a lot of books, where you can always find refuge and privacy from the world. You can be sitting in a chair and go anywhere you like.

One of my coworkers, I'll call him Jason, collected reptiles: snakes and bearded dragons, geckos and other lizards. I don't remember why, but his pets were delivered to work, where they'd arrive in a heavy box that moved in the hands of the delivery person, who looked confused and ready to be free of whatever was in there and probably wondering what kind of bookstore this was. Jason was not supposed to accept live animal deliveries at work, obviously, but the manager didn't know, and nobody told on him. Still, we had to keep the box out of sight, so we put the critters behind the register, still in their boxes, beneath our feet. I wondered what a devoted reptile keeper might do to the person who let Diana the snake, for example, escape into the chaos of the food court, but Jason was nice to me and used to call me "a walking sunset," which was a bit creepy but didn't seem cause for alarm. Inside the box I felt the animal moving around, saw an occasional flash of scales or spots in the air holes. I found it thrilling to be reading a book or completing a transaction and feel a little movement, a tiny shudder beneath my toes, or a big jump when the cash register sounded. It was like having a secret, *and* it was breaking a rule, and the rule was often a *snake*, and nobody got hurt; the reptiles continued to their forever home with Jason.

The writer Stephen Graham Jones once told my students, "Art is about breaking things. Break everything." Writing isn't *always* about breaking the rules, but sometimes it is absolutely that. Sometimes you bring a snake to work. Doing something new in art—maybe something you've been told you can't or shouldn't—is frightening, empowering, frustrating, *and* fulfilling. The scripts we've been given that were never true and are no longer resonant, the stories told about us that we refuse to believe any longer, can be challenged, remade, dispatched, even flipped—this is an artist's daily work, the work of a life. Mining life experiences for meaning—no matter their tenor or intensity—acts as the ultimate epistemological compass, and as we come to know ourselves better, we understand how to make art that will serve the world in some way. The richness, truth, tragedy, and triumph of a life transmuted into art serves the artist, but it also serves others—it might even save them.

From the life material you are given—no matter how messy or radiant—you can make something beautiful and true that will be received by another in ways you might anticipate and in ways you never could have imagined. Maybe someone will hate it—but this, too, is an emotional response and means you have held up a mirror to someone and they didn't like the reflection, which is not a reflection on you, but on the viewer. Your art is alive and bothering people! Great. You've done your job. Your art makes someone decide to live another day in the world. Yay. Job well done. This, to me, is the greatest exchange, that great conversation holding the world together in mysterious ways we can feel and sense if we allow ourselves to do this. Rachel Naomi Remen writes, "The places in which we are seen and heard are holy places." This counteracts what Tara Brach describes as our "deepest longing," which is "for belonging," and a sense of belonging is often difficult to feel, to seek, to find.

When you make art, you belong to the world—not because you proved yourself worthy, but because you don't need to. You have always belonged. Through art, we can walk that tightrope of alienation or pass through those tight spaces where we feel lost; stories create the nets that catch us, the hands that reach into the pit and offer us a way to climb out. I often think of my daughter standing on the Dragon's Teeth of Maui, fully believing that by talking to the waves she could harness them and bend them to her eight-year-old will. "C'mon wave," she'd say, making a dramatic pulling motion with her hands as if she could move the wave closer, a little ginger witchy princess harnessing the power and movement of water and wind because she imagined, which is to say believed, that it was entirely within her power—maybe not fully, but part of her did, because she owned the role completely. When a wave crashed in just the way she was moving her hands, she bellowed up to the sky, to whom- or whatever, "THANK YOU!" The very picture of creative freedom and ideas being co-created with the input that is available to us in the world at any time, if only we're open enough to recognize it, name it, believe it, and be grateful for it.

Meditation teacher Jack Kornfield speaks often about "the mystery of incarnation." Yeah, no shit. A mystery and a lot of work. It's hard to have a body; it's hard to be a person; it's hard to be hopeful; it's hard to make art in a world that is always on fire or about to be. But it's not impossible. Art can help you, in forms that you're "good" at, and forms that you're not and never will be, to find meaning and purpose in your days. It's about the act of doing it, or "the process" as writers are fond of saying, but that always makes me think of a meat processing plant, which isn't a great image.

One winter a few years ago, in the lead-up to the ten-year anniversary of my son's death, I felt heartbroken about everything, and also numb and floaty and slow. I did what a lot of middle-aged white women do (not pickleball, although I do walk in a weighted vest): ayahuasca and magic mushrooms.

The shaman, A, blew the medicine into my nose with a little wooden pipe, and then I swallowed several big doses of magic mushrooms at various intervals, and we did holotropic breathing in between. She played drums and other instruments, and I emerged about six hours later after growing wings on the floor and flying up into a dome of light. Yep. For years I'd been poking fun at people who went to Peru to get enlightened. I wasn't in Peru, I was in an apartment in South Los Angeles, but it was awesome and emotional and exhausting and liberating. At the end of our session, which also included visions of spiders, cathedral windows, and someone beating a big bass drum in one corner, A asked me to make artwork about my experience.

She handed me a sheet of paper, and I wrote down some words that literally moved and jumped on the page, as if the page had fleas. "I always knew words were alive!" I said gleefully. A came over to have a look.

"Try again," she said.

I wrote more words while she waited. The late-afternoon sun was moving through her singing bowls, which I had to watch for a moment before I could respond. "I'm a writer," I explained. "Words are how I *see things*." I was still in a trippy, disoriented space, but I was also very sincere.

"Okay," she said. "Let's try something else."

A crouched in front of me and asked me to look into her eyes.

"Uh . . . what?" The walls were still melting into the floor, and now we were eye-gazing?

"Do it," she said, but kindly, and so I did.

She started pounding on my chest with her fist. "Repeat

after me," she said. "I love my body. I am a beautiful artist. I love myself. I forgive myself. I am a beautiful artist." I couldn't say it the first twenty or maybe eighty times she asked me—I lost track. I felt like she'd been pounding on my chest for nearly an hour, and when I managed to say it very softly, I started to cry like I don't think I've ever cried in my life. I've spent so much of my life hating my body, not because of what it could do or how it felt to be in it—both of which I enjoyed—but how the world treated it, saw it, recoiled from the difference of it, or labeled it as "inspiring" for no real reason. Evoking fear in others or anticipating that one might do so is one of the most alienating feelings in the world, and the popularity of *Frankenstein*, hundreds of years after its publication, proves that other people feel this way too. I understood that art had saved me, and I didn't need to prove anything to anyone or even to myself; I just needed to keep doing it.

When my sobbing receded, A said, "Now try drawing again." This time I did what I often do when I'm teaching: I made rudimentary stick figure art. I put cones around stick figures to talk about Tornado Theory; I drew fuzzy lines on the board to talk about horizons; I drew circles and bows and more stick figures doing more things to illustrate the thing a writer might be trying to do in a story, or to illustrate one way of approaching that story. The picture—in pink pen—looked like it was made by a four-year-old or found on the wall of a cave somewhere.

"Perfect," A said. "Now you've got it." I've never felt embarrassed by my art again; the truth is, any visual works as an illustration, and it doesn't need to be "good" to communicate the meaning behind it. I'm also unlikely to ever "get better" as a visual artist, so I can stay roaming around in the magical Eden of beginner's mind, naked and not at all self-conscious. A spacious mind is one that's connected to intelligence and kindness—a sky-like mind. It's a place and space where a light grasp—on everything—can lead to a huge artistic leap that might change your life, and possibly someone else's too.

Tennessee Williams is credited with this bit of wisdom, and it rings true, regardless of whether or not he said it:

> The world is violent and mercurial—it will have its way with you. We are saved only by love—love for each other and the love that we pour into the art we feel compelled to share: being a parent; being a writer; being a partner; being a friend. We live in a perpetually burning building, and what we must save from it, all the time, is love.

Love is the inexhaustible resource that is transmuted by our horizons of meaning, creating connections with the living, the dead, and ourselves.

I was once sitting with my student Mark, discussing his pages, when he turned to me and said, "You surprise me. After all you've been through, you're such a delightful person." I nearly choked on my California roll. This is not how I see myself, and many people I've known (or dated or been married to) would violently disagree with this statement, which is part of what makes it so funny. But Mark's comment had some truth to it: my life as an artist has made me happy, maybe happier than some because I know it is possible to be the kind of sad that you are sure will kill you and then it doesn't, and you live. *I would die if I were you.* No, you probably wouldn't, but maybe you might at some point say, *I found a way to live happily,* not ever after, but for now, and in a way that you might not have chosen but can still be your own and still bring you joy. I was happier than I've been in over a decade while writing this book, which is exploring how to make art and meaning during or after or about the worst experiences of your life. Art heals you; you heal others through art—by that I mean flip scripts, break patterns, interrogate all narratives, question all statements that begin with *It must be like this.* Any project is bigger than the making of it—through whatever difficulties or blocks arise. Remaking the world can sustain you through just about anything. This still surprises me.

As creators, we tell stories, and these stories hold the light we're charged to seek, keep, nourish, cultivate, and share, even and especially within chaos. That's our job. We live in a radical, radiant, split-apart, and fiery world, and we need radical writing and art—brave, open, intelligent, demanding. It's not a small job, but it's also a choice: the only person hiring you is you. Be a good boss, be a good worker, find joy in what you're doing even if it feels like welcoming terror.

What sets a book or a painting or a song or a photograph apart is simple and unique and complex and unrepeatable: *you.* You're the one doing the writing, performing, singing, capturing. Whoever you are, only you can bring that person—that architect—to the page. All stories are about surviving in order to belong, or belonging in order to survive. So be a radical witness to the world and to your life within it. Not a judge, but a witness who is radically aware of the connectivity of every person who has ever lived. It is that epic. Allow your curiosity to be the brightness that illuminates the unknown, shadowy spaces you may face, or the hidden places in your heart that you thought held shameful secrets, but in the end hold only stories. There's nothing to fear, only something to know, even if it's never fully understood. Stop walking on eggshells around your art; nobody wants an eggshell omelet, so crack some real eggs.

You, be nice to my friend. Be an adult but think like a child. Bring your reptile to work. Relax your grip. Unclench your butthole. Don't wait for a personal trauma to make your last fucks fly; set them free now through the floating window in the sky. If you do know tragedy, use it. Leverage it. Get curious and uncomfortable and see who you are and what you made when you come out on the other side. Let your art be the anchor you lift for the ship that carries a lost stranger where they need to go or are afraid to go but must. Shine a light in the places where there is none: that is our task. Stories cast light, and we are the light bearers. Name it to frame it, frame it to bear it, not to bury it or misplace it or give someone else a burden, but to give them a lamp. You only need one. Set your lantern on the water and let it disappear to parts unknown. Let your art be the life you reimagine, for you, for the people you love and those you've lost, and for the beautiful, complicated strangers you'll never meet but who will know you because you *did the thing and you are one of us.*

Go forth. Be of service.

ACKNOWLEDGMENTS

No book takes shape without the minds and hearts of many dedicated people working together: artists, families, students, colleagues, and friends. I am grateful to the Corporation of Yaddo, for yet again making possible a year's worth of work in only two weeks. Thank you, Tara Ison, for reminding me that our mistakes are just the actions of people being human. Thank you to my colleagues at UC Riverside, especially Katie Ford, Alex Espinoza, Allison Hedge Coke, and Tod Goldberg. Your support and kindness and brilliance are unparalleled. Thank you to my wonderful, brilliant, and kind agent, Dorian Karchmar, who continues to believe in me. Thanks to the hardworking and loveliest of editors, Dan Smetanka, who nurtured this seed of an idea into a book. Thank you to Leela Corman, for making physically manifest what lives in the hearts of grieving moms. Thank you to Gina Frangello, my badass bestie, chosen sister, unpaid therapist, text editor, adventure buddy, and partner in all literary and bookish pursuits. Thank you to Julie Coyne, my spiritual sister and compassionate guide, who has given me a place in Guatemala along with an understanding of an expansive love that I never would have known without her. Thank you to "Gilmore Girls daughter" Annemarie Hauser, the tallest girl with the biggest, purest heart who will always be a part of my family. Thank you to my brother James, for making and keeping promises, and for being the wisest and most ethical person I know, and to my brother-in-law, Robby, for being literally the best cook and host in the history of the world. Thank you to Ryann Watson-Stites, for dancing with me in our dorm room. Thank you to my parents, Roger and Mary (a.k.a. Oger and Mar-Dog), who have had my back all my life, and who continue to put up with me and say encouraging words, even if they don't understand what I'm doing about 75 percent of the time. Thank you to Rob Roberge, for the music-making and our pact and #shitrobsays and for being such a good dude. Thanks to my Redlands crew—Margaret Ohayon, Robin Jennings, KC and Natalie Hohensee, and Susana Crespo—for helping with the logistical issues of having a young child while navigating the life of a mother, a writer, and a person. Thank you to Monika Bustamante and Chris Simpson, for being a Texas home away from home. Thank you to my Boston ride or dies and *wicked smaht* beauties: Kate Weldon LeBlanc and Jennifer Weber. Thank you to Cynthia Schwartz for being my enthusiastic champion and for remembering my boy so faithfully. Thank you to Lisa Glatt and David Hernandez, for "getting it" and Long Beach shenanigans. Thank you to Joni Green, for keeping my body able and strong and prepared for the zombie apocalypse. Thanks to Matthew Zapruder, for the funniest text threads ever, and to Bret Anthony Johnston, for always saying yes to "Oh hey, this is last minute but . . ." Thanks to Emily Miles—I'm so glad our chance meeting in Geneva has led to all these decades of friendship. Thank you to Sarah Woods, for "betweenity." Thank you to Kay Tolchin, the most generous person I know, for giving me space and time and encouragement when I needed it most, in some of the most extraordinary places on earth, and for her genius editorial prowess. Thank you to Ruth Krah, for making sure my house doesn't collapse under the weight of its messiness. Thank you to the Loss Ladies, for helping me find creative ways to tell difficult stories. Thank you to the healers in my life: Alex and Ro and Leanne and Athanasia.

Thank you to those who said I couldn't do this or that, which inspired me to do exactly those things.

Thank you to my many teachers and mentors over the years: Barbara Pitkin, David Bradley, Edmund Santurri, Frank Ostaseski, Tara Brach, and so many others, including those who are no longer living and those I've never met. Your words and wisdom live on in books and experiences, across time and history and experience and this temporal sphere.

Thank you to my students, from all times and spaces and places. You are the reason this book exists, and you have made my life as a teacher joyous, challenging, inspiring, meaningful, and deep. And fun! Please always tell me what you're doing and send me postcards (Thank you, Kelsey Ferrell!) and let me celebrate all the wins with you. I can't wait to see what you do next.

Finally, thank you to my children, Ronan and Charlie.

Because of you, my life is bright, big, complicated, exquisite, adventurous, loving, luminous, tender, and the only one I'd ever want to live. My babies. My two North Stars.

October 25, 2025
Tecate, Mexico

APPENDIX

These exercises and strategies and considerations—many of which are inspired by my students over two decades—are meant to assist you in building, maintaining, and finding joy in your creative practice. The fabric of your life is all you need, along with a willingness to explore what makes it uniquely yours, and how you might share it with others and the world. Reminder: There's no way to do it "right." There's no way to get it "wrong."

Manuscript Glow-Up: Read Your Work Aloud

Storytelling is an oral form—the Greeks knew this, poets still do, and now so do you. You can replicate the experience of telling stories around the fire as they did in days of yore by doing this particular exercise, no camping required. When you read your work aloud, you will catch bumps and awkward sentences in a way you never will when reading your work on paper or especially on the computer screen. I have a very specific way that I like to do this: it's awful, you won't like it, and it's totally worth it. When my students do this exercise, they disappear for about two weeks, during which they are probably pushing pins into a voodoo doll shaped like me, and then they reemerge to tell me, without fail, that it was the most helpful editorial technique ever. Of all time. Because it is.

1. Print out your latest, current draft. The one that's as complete as possible *for now.*
2. Read the whole manuscript aloud into a recording device of some kind. I have an old Dictaphone from the nineties that uses tiny tapes I keep recording over. A phone works too. In this step, you are *not allowed* to make any notes or changes. Trust me, you will want to. But don't. Just read it aloud that way the book is in this particular moment in time, at this point in its evolution.
3. This is the worst but most important step, in part because it's like listening to an answering machine message of your voice for hours on end, for those of us who remember listening to our voices echo through an apartment after the *beep* when someone called and nobody was interested in answering. Listen to the recording, with the manuscript in hand, and *now* you can start cutting and making notes. Stop the recording when you need to make a change and then start it up again. This is the most time-intensive of the three steps, but it's the most revealing and useful; it's also uncomfortable and carries a serious cringe factor. You'll find so many tiny errors, big bumps, and repetitions you didn't even know you had when

you do this. The next draft will be cleaner, more polished, leveled up. Added bonus: you will never be the writer who is asked to read for ten minutes and then reads for an hour. You're welcome.

That's an Essay! The Game Show

My friend Tod Goldberg, a writer, calls me the "frozen yogurt machine of essays," in the sense that I have been writing nonfiction for so long that I can identify anecdotes that, if tugged on and untangled a bit, might make powerful essays. In other words, pull the lever on the Froyo machine, get a cool and delicious treat. Although it's not that simple, looking for essays in the everyday is an interesting way to engage with and experience the world. How do you do this? When people talk, listen. Deeply listen. Don't be crafting your reply, or thinking about what they think of you, or doing anything else but listening. It's often in conversation—with ourselves and others—that our best ideas are born, but we must pay attention in order for these ideas to breathe and evolve. I've developed a habit over the years of proclaiming, "That's an essay!" when a student (or anyone, really) starts talking about an issue or subject or moment that mattered to them, an experience with deep and interesting layers that I'd be interested in learning more about. Scout for essays the way a talent agency searches for models or movie people look for film locations. The more you practice identifying essays in the wild, the better you'll get at it. Some of the ideas might turn out to be duds, but others won't, and that's part of the process too. Imagine you are the host of a game show when you meet someone new or have coffee with someone you know; listen with your full attention to what they're telling you about the details of their lives—the mundane and the magnificent. There's always a narrative weave between the two, and identifying those connections is what makes personal story layered, impactful, and universal. When you detect this convergence, your friend wins the game show and you can holler, "That's an essay!"

Imagine Your Ideal Audience

Who are you writing for? Who is your ideal reader or viewer or listener? Who are your people? It's okay that not everybody will be interested in your book (or you). Being a writer is not about people-pleasing, and it's also not about waiting for external gratification, which is the processed sugar of communication—you'll only crave more, and only a little bit is good for you. Remember: ego inflation and ego deflation are both disrupters of your peace, and peace is the goal. I ask my students who their audience is all the time and remind them that there's no judgment in who is in that imagined audience. These are your people, your imagined readers or viewers or listeners, so you're calling all the shots. One of my former graduate students, Kelsey Ferrell, thought of this amazing theater metaphor in response to this question:

> I like to think about my audience not as a group of invisible readers, but the actual rows inside a theater.

In the front row, you have the people who are tried-and-true fans—they showed up early to make sure they got that front-row seat. These are also the ones who align so closely with your work that you might get tunnel vision about their presence, thinking this is the only audience you have. But this neglects the other rows. The people who showed up with a general admission ticket and found a spot in the middle of the auditorium. The people who stood in the doorway at the very back, who are peeking in and thinking about finding a seat. If you only write for that front row, you'll miss inviting the doorway readers in. Oftentimes we cater to who we know already enjoys us. It was easy for me to tell myself I wrote for young, educated, ambitious women and think that I was hitting the nail on the head. Having one sentence to describe your audience is great for query letters, but not great for when you're actually writing. My writing got better when I told myself the young, educated, ambitious women were already seated in my front row. What I really needed to do was welcome a larger group. Nowadays, I try to lasso in the doorway readers. I try to convince those sitting in general admission for one project to come back for the next. It allows me to be surprised about who my audience is, and puts me in the growth mindset that I can always invite more people in. Furthermore, it dissolves the oversimplified thinking that usually falls along identitarian lines, breaking the pattern of

> thinking our readers are just like us. There are many ways you can add to this metaphor and start thinking about who's really in the theater: Who's seated in the balcony? Who's working the snack bar and might overhear the show? Ask yourself these questions. Not only will your writing become richer, but the pressure to please the front row and never risk alienating them will also fade once it clicks that they're not the only pillar your work stands on.

This notion of a tiered audience idea is interesting and fun, requiring discernment, humility, and a deep understanding that it's okay not to appeal to everyone. Based on Kelsey's description, ask yourself: Who is in the front row, who is in the middle, who is in the nosebleeds, who is heckling from the balcony, and who wandered into the wrong theater and doesn't know what to do but might possibly be convinced to stay? And remember, your audience changes and evolves as you change and evolve. You can do this exercise for any project at any time.

Outside Artist

> *Above all else, it is about leaving a mark that I existed: I was here. I was hungry. I was defeated. I was happy. I was sad. I was in love. I was afraid. I was hopeful. I had an idea and I had a good purpose and that's why I made works of art.*
>
> —Felix Gonzalez-Torres

Felix Gonzalez-Torres believed that the wall between museum and world, outer and inner experience, was permeable. His art is designed to move outside all walls and into the experience of living people, not in a prescriptive way but in an expansive and connective way. My brother James describes Felix's art this way:

> Felix craved conversion and change for this world, for us. He knew one rarely happens without the other. And that they dance, intertwined, inseparable—and he selflessly never wanted to be the conversation or the change himself. His art is a catalyst. It's in our interaction with it that we meet ourselves and one another. It mattered. Well, it first mattered when he was young and hopeful. Then it mattered as a lesion appeared on his body, and then another, and the realization that we die. We die before we are ever done, mostly. Sometimes we die because we are done. It mattered because it wasn't about him. He scrubbed himself from his art (long before the internet created a digital fingerprint of ourselves we can never erase) so that we might, perchance, experience ourselves, experience the other.

Art is a great conversation, a lifelong collaboration with the self, with others, and with the world across time and history, which is extraordinary. Why should your art abide by ordinary rules? Think imaginatively about how your art engages with and emerges within the world, and how it might reach people in unexpected, delightful, or disturbing ways. What do you want people to take away, into their minds and hearts? For Felix, it was pieces of candy or sheets of paper from his artwork that were taken into the world to tell new stories and create more connections—known or unknown. Imagine your work being absorbed by the world. Not monetized or weaponized or sanctified, just absorbed, cataloged into the mind and heart and body in ways that you will never know, but that will have ripple effects in every area of your life. What work do you think your art might be doing that dissolves the perceived wall between self and other? What might be a visual or musical or outward-facing representation of that movement? Write a poem and leave it on a coffee shop table. Maybe someone will throw it away, maybe they won't. Sing a song on your porch loud enough so the dog walkers can hear you. Make something and give it to a child, to a stranger, to a person you haven't talked to in a decade but have been thinking about.

Immersive Beginnings and Open Endings

How do you want the reader to feel when they start a book, a chapter, a paragraph? Think about how you want the reader to feel *in their body* at the beginning, and what might remain unsaid at the end, which will evoke a different feeling. Writing is embodied; we register feelings in our bodies first, not after they've gone through an intellectual organizational process. For example, if someone walks up to you and says, "You're a horrible person," you don't think, *Oh, they called me horrible and now I feel bad*; you feel instantly ashamed, which might register in your body as cold hands and hot cheeks, a shortness of breath or a heaviness in your feet. Readers also have bodies and when you write you are creating an embodied experience for them as well, and because bodies remember everything even when our minds don't, it's a great place to start.

Do you want the beginning to feel like a cold plunge or a slow lowering into a saltwater pool with the perfect temperature? Try to avoid beginning in a state of what I call to-ing and fro-ing, in the transit part of the scene, when the heart of the scene happens five whole minutes later. Do we need the drive from the house to the airport? If so, there'd better be one hell of a conversation or vivid argument happening in that car. You don't need to show us collecting your bag in baggage claim—even if it's a very interesting airport in a far-flung destination that makes you look cool and well traveled on social media—unless your bag has a bomb in it or something very dramatic is happening vis-à-vis your checked luggage. We've all been to airports. We've all picked up our bags. Plop us down in the place we're going and then start the scene there. Or give us a slow on-ramp and give us a beautiful line as an opening gesture. Or grab us by the hand and pull us through the portal before we can change our minds about whether or not to keep reading.

You know when you reach the end of a book or a great television show and feel sad because you're no longer experiencing life alongside the characters? That's a sign of great storytelling. It's also why I've read *War and Peace* so many times or watched every episode of *NYPD Blue* ten times. Endings should make the reader want to keep reading, but they don't need to because the characters are so fully alive. What's the feeling you want to end on and let the reader take with them out into the world?

Give Your Book a Shape

Giving your book a shape during its construction is somewhat of an abstraction, but a useful one. Like an adverb, you want to use an abstraction sparingly, so the instruction is not to give your book ten shapes but just the one, and it's most useful to identify a simple one that might mean many things but actually means or represents a *very particular* thing to you. You need ONE organizing image and it does not have to make logical sense to you. Magic defies logic. A dream is a dream *because* it's realistic, not definitely achievable. As usual, the first image that comes to you is the one to trust.

I started doing this exercise with my third book, *Sanctuary*, which has a great deal of information about Viking ships and boats in general. I wanted the reader to feel as if they were being rocked in a simple boat on water that wasn't calm and still but also wasn't so turbulent that the journey was frightening. I wanted people to feel alert and held, so I imagined an old sturdy canoe on a gently rippling lake. Ask yourself: If I had to assign my book a shape, a container, what would it look like? Trust what emerges. Trust the intentions of your intuition. Trust that if the shape makes no sense now, it might later.

Five Moments of Rupture

Rupture is a line-in-the-sand moment, a moment when everything shifts, the experience that generates a *before* and an *after*. It can be a moment of great sadness or tremendous joy—anything that marks a shift that can never shift back, a disruption, a permanent change. A diagnosis, a divorce, an accident, falling in love or falling out of it, getting or losing a job, any loss or gain. When we're asked about the most important moments in our lives, we often respond with big milestones like marriage or the birth of children or a new job, degree, skill, or a divorce, a gutting loss, a diagnosis. These are important, but your subconscious has more tiny, intimate moments it wants to bring out, filaments of experience—the web that holds the spider. I do this exercise whenever I'm starting something or stuck in the middle of something. What's great about this exercise is that it uses the now of your thoughts (the moments falling from your head in this particular moment in time), and then your memory of them. Two realms of time are invoked: *chronos* and *kairos*. Now you're crossing time, space, and memory in whatever you're writing, creating rich layers of meaning within the narrative with a minimal amount of effort and overthinking. Win-win!

1. If you had to tell the story of this book, your life, this chapter, in only five moments, what would they be? Write down the first five moments that fall out of your mind, even if they seem weird or completely random.

2. Address each moment in the order in which it arrived from the beautiful engine of your brain. Spend fifteen to forty-five minutes (forty-five is ideal) doing a massive sensory dump of everything connected to that moment: sights, sounds, smells, the way the air felt on your skin, what someone might have said. It doesn't have to make sense; it might just be words and sounds and memories. Don't judge it. Keep going. Do this for each of the five moments. Write by hand, make voice notes, type. Whatever works for you and will allow you to feel free to accept what comes forth and nonjudgmental about what you're generating.
3. Set the pages aside for a few days, a week, a month. Then go back and see what connections your mind made when you weren't stressing it out with commands like WRITE THIS CHAPTER WELL OR YOU SUCK, when you were just trusting the contents of your brain and allowing the intuition we're all born with to provoke lines and memories and images and bits of story. Find the connection. There will be so many—some of them will surprise you; others will delight or distress you. Trust me. Trust yourself. And while there will be plenty of big milestones, there will be tiny ones too: the ones you didn't remember or didn't want to, old memories dusted off and ready to rumble, an insight about the situation that is fresh and fascinating.

Window to the World

Windows are portals through which we watch, wait, and wonder. Think of Leandro Erlich's floating window as a jumping-off (or through) point. How many times have you sat behind a window, waiting for someone to arrive or leave, or wondering about your life? When I was six years old and terrified that my mother was going to die every time she left the house, I'd plant myself on the love seat and stare out the window until she returned. When I had insomnia, I'd sit in front of the window and watch snow fall like dust through the darkness. Waiting for love, waiting for a job, waiting for inspiration, for sleep, for a return. This exercise helps with world-building, interiority, and crossing time.

1. Imagine someone walking by your house and looking inside. What would they see and how might they interpret that scene? Would they see a family sitting down for dinner happily, while in fact the parents have just had an argument and nobody is speaking? Would they see a person eating alone, which may seem sad but if they were in the room they'd understand that person was perfectly happy eating their muesli alone and reading a book? Think of the creature in *Frankenstein*, who peered into windows, gutted with sadness, wishing he could be a part of a family, aching to belong. What do you see when you walk along a street at night and catch a glimpse of what's going on through a lit window? What we see isn't

always the truth. What we think we want isn't always what will make us happy.

2. Place yourself in a room where you are looking through a window. This place could be an office, a kitchen, an airplane. How does what you see outside impact your interior thoughts and feelings? How does what you're looking out over describe or circumscribe your life in some way? Maybe there's a tree you planted when your first child was born, and now they're in college, a sign of time passing. Maybe you see a row of trees, and all the activity of squirrels and birds in their branches, and this makes you grateful or calm. Maybe you look out the window at a road and wish you could be on it and then ask yourself why.
3. Thinking of Erlich's sculpture, what is a metaphorical window for you? What experience took you more deeply into your feelings or your life in a way you didn't anticipate? Perhaps it was a new partner, or lover, or friend, or collaborator. Perhaps it was a piece of art that made you think about a time in your life that made you think about this time in the world, and now you're ready to make some connections and play That's an Essay! The Game Show.

What Would You Steal and What Do You Feel?

The workshop model of critique can start to feel a bit stale if you spend decades doing it, as I have. While considerations of what's working and what's not working, and questions like "What's your favorite moment or line?" are useful and thought-provoking, there are other ways to initiate meaningful conversations among artists and writers. When possible, instead of writing formal papers or long letters of critique, I ask my students to answer these two questions about a published work or sometimes the work of their peers: What would you steal? And what do you feel? Simple questions, but the answers are often more evocative than "what's working is . . ." or anything that starts with the phrase "I liked." Manuscripts are living things through which intimate human interactions are made possible. When I read a book that I cannot put down, I often think, *Wow, I wish I'd written that* in an awestruck way. Once you're fully committed to your art and happily doing it, jealousy will be revealed as the waste-of-time lie that it is.

PROJECT PLAYLIST

> *A book—or an album—is a network of thought, pinching together events and impressions to form a narrative or a lattice of time.*
>
> —Heather McCalden, from *The Observable Universe*

I started making playlists for my students' essays—tracks or whole records I was listening to while I read their work, or tracks I thought of while reading their work and then listened to later. They loved it, so I kept doing it for them, and then started doing it with my own work. This exercise works well with the Give Your Book a Shape exercise. Here, a playlist or a series of songs creates a sonic container and casts a musical mood for the work. This is helpful because all containers require a necessary discernment to create a boundary, and it's also a soundtrack you can play whenever you're working on the book, which establishes a mind/sound groove that can be both motivating and reassuring. When you work on the book, you listen to its soundtrack.

This Book's Playlist (on Shuffle)

"So Good at Being in Trouble," Unknown Mortal Orchestra
"DNA.," Kendrick Lamar
"Modern Living," Mountain Time
"This Is America," Childish Gambino
"Song of Unborn," Steven Wilson
"Harvest Moon," Neil Young
"Jesus: The Missing Years," John Prine
"Attitude," Bad Brains
"GTFOMF," Big Freedia
"Porgi, amor," from *The Marriage of Figaro*, Mozart
"Workinonit," J Dilla
"Dirt Woman Blues," Grainne Duffy
"Guided by Wire," Neko Case
"Respect," Alliance Ethnik
"Famine," Sinéad O'Connor
"House Work," Jax Jones
"Sabotage," Beastie Boys
"Ronan," Taylor Swift
"Major Tom," Peter Schilling
"I'll Sail This Ship Alone," the Beautiful South
"Freedom," Pharrell Williams
"Vivrant Thing," Q-Tip
"The Flower Called Nowhere," Stereolab
"Do You Realize??," the Flaming Lips

BIBLIOGRAPHY

The Fire Next Time, James Baldwin

Radical Acceptance: Embracing Your Life with the Heart of a Buddha, Tara Brach

The Chaneysville Incident, David Bradley

When Things Fall Apart, Pema Chödrön

"PTSD: The Wound That Never Heals," Leela Corman

The Brothers Karamazov, Fyodor Dostoevsky

The Disabled God: Toward a Liberatory Theology of Disability, Nancy L. Eiesland

Deposition and *Blood Lyrics*, Katie Ford

Blow Your House Down: A Story of Family, Feminism, and Treason, Gina Frangello

Who Wrote the Bible?, Richard Elliott Friedman

Truth and Method, Hans-Georg Gadamer

The Wild Iris, Louise Glück

High-Risk Homosexual, Edgar Gomez

The Doors of the Sea: Where Was God in the Tsunami?, David Bentley Hart

The Phenomenology of Spirit, Georg Wilhelm Friedrich Hegel

All About Love, bell hooks

The Varieties of Religious Experience, William James

We Burn Daylight, Bret Anthony Johnston

Mongrels, Stephen Graham Jones

Letters to Milena, Franz Kafka

In Face of Mystery: A Constructive Theology, Gordon D. Kaufman

Fear and Trembling, Søren Kierkegaard

The Complete Nag Hammadi Scriptures: Lost Gospels, Secret Teachings, and the Hidden Roots of Early Christianity, Ezra Malakim

Wolf Hall, *Bring Up the Bodies*, and *The Mirror & the Light*, Hilary Mantel

The Observable Universe, Heather McCalden

The Genealogy of Morals, Friedrich Nietzsche

The Grieving Brain: The Surprising Science of How We Learn from Love and Loss, Mary-Frances O'Connor

The Five Invitations: Discovering What Death Can Teach Us About Living Fully, Frank Ostaseski

Liar, Rob Roberge

Frankenstein; or, The Modern Prometheus, Mary Shelley

Extraordinary Bodies: Figuring Physical Disability in American Culture and Literature, Rosemarie Garland Thomson

War and Peace, Leo Tolstoy

A Life in Letters, Simone Weil

To the Lighthouse, Virginia Woolf

COMMUNITY AS ART

Much of this book has been about the power of community as it relates to nurturing creativity. Artistic nourishment comes from so many communal sources, and in some cases, the love and care expressed through these communities is its own art form. Below are two of the places and people and communities that have sustained me as an artist and a person.

Education and Hope is an example of what love in action looks like, empowering and nourishing children and families in rural Guatemala. E and H is a container of love, support, and hope like none other. educationandhope.org/.

National Tay-Sachs & Allied Diseases Association supports the families of children living with Tay-Sachs and other terminal illnesses. The mothers and families I met during Ronan's illness were a literal lifeline for me and remain so for children currently living with these terminal conditions. ntsad.org/.

These are my communities, based on my interests and experiences, but one of the best things a creative person can do is find ways to be creative and curious within a community. Learning how to support and be supported, honor vulnerability in yourself and others, and work toward a common cause will feed your writing and your life equally.

© William Waldron

EMILY RAPP BLACK is the author of the *New York Times* bestsellers *Poster Child*, *The Still Point of the Turning World*, *Sanctuary*, and *Frida Kahlo and My Left Leg*. A former Fulbright Scholar and Guggenheim Fellow, and a graduate of Harvard Divinity School, she is a professor of creative writing at University of California–Riverside, where she also teaches in the School of Medicine.